AF619324

MADHYA PRADESH

A STATE STUDY GUIDE

RAHUL SINGH

Published by

Hawk Press

4836/24, Ansari Road, Daryaganj
New Delhi – 110 002
Phones: 91-11-23278618, 91-11-43667199
E-mail: thehawkpress@gmail.com
www.thehawkpress.com

ISBN: 978-93-88318-71-6

Preface

The history of Madhya Pradesh goes back to the time of Ashoka, the great Mauryan ruler. Major portion of Central India formed part of the Gupta Empire (300-550 AD). In the first half of the seventh century it was part of domains of famous emperor Harsha. The close of tenth century was a period of confusion. In the early eleventh century the muslims entered central India, First Mahmud of Ghazni & then Mohammad Gori who incorporated certain parts with Sultanate of Delhi. It also formed part of Mughal empire with the rise of Maratha's. Till the death of Madhoji Scindia in 1794, Marathas ruled supreme in Central India, but after that independent & smaller states came into being. The disintegrated smaller states paved way for British suzerainty. Some great women rulers like Rani Ahilyabai Holkar of Indore, Gond queen Rani Kamla devi & Rani Durgawati have carved a nick for them in history.

The area covered by the present-day Madhya Pradesh includes the area of the ancient Avanti Mahajanapada, whose capital Ujjain(also known as Avantika) arose as a major city during the second wave of Indian urbanisation in the sixth century BCE. Subsequently, the region was ruled by the major dynasties of India. By the early 18th century, the region was divided into several small kingdoms which were captured by the British and incorporated into Central Provinces and Berar and the Central India Agency. After India's independence, Madhya Pradesh state was created with Nagpur as its capital: this state included the southern parts of the present-day Madhya Pradesh and northeastern portion of today's

Maharashtra. In 1956, this state was reorganised and its parts were combined with the states of Madhya Bharat, Vindhya Pradesh and Bhopal to form the new Madhya Pradesh state, the Marathi-speaking Vidarbha region was removed and merged with the then Bombay State. This state was the largest in India by area until 2000, when its southeastern Chhattisgarh region was made as a separate state.

When India became independent in 1947, the British Indian province of Central Provinces and Berar formed Madhya Pradesh. Boundary changes followed; the state of Chhattisgarh was carved out of Madhya Pradesh.

Madhya Pradesh, as its name implies, lies in the heart of India, whose topography ranges from plateau with the Vindhya & the Satpura mountain ranges, the plains in the east, meandering rivers, rocky hills & ravines to lush green forests. State offers all important pillars of Indian tourism like pilgrim tourism, wildlife tourism, heritage tourism, buddhism, adventure sports etc.

This is a reference book. All the matter is just compiled and edited in nature, taken from the various sources which are in public domain.

This book is endeavours to present before the readers a panoramic view of the state, its districts, places, cultures, arts and crafts, developmental policies, economy along with history of dynasties that ruled the state.

—*Editor*

ABOUT THE BOOK

Madhya Pradesh is commonly abbreviated as M.P. in India local. Its name "Madhya Pradesh" means "Central Region" because is if located at Central of India in plains. Till year 2000, Madhya Pradesh was the largest state of India in area-wise but after creation of Chattisgarh state from Madhya Pradesh area, it become second largest state in area-wise and 6th largest state in population wise. Is is among few states of India who shares their state border with other states of India and not with any other country or coastal line. Its north-east border touches Uttar Pradesh state, north-west border touches Rajasthan, western border touches Gujarat, south-west border touches Maharashtra state and south-east border touches Chattisgarh. After Independence, all the states signed the instruments of accession in to the Indian Union & on 28th May, 1948 a new state, Madhya Bharat came into existence with Indore & Gwalior as its capital. In the north, as the result of merger of 35 princely states of Bundelkhand & Baghelkhand, Vindhya Pradesh cane into being in April 1948 & in 1952, an elected ministry was formed with Rewa as its capital. Madhya Pradesh is a state in the India. This book is endeavours to present before the readers a panoramic view of the state, its districts, places, cultures, arts and crafts, developmental policies, economy along with history of dynasties that ruled the state.

Contents

	Preface	*(iii)*
1.	State at a Glance	1
2.	Culture and Society	20
3.	Government and Politics	44
4.	Language and Literature	58
5.	Geography and Flora & Fauna	63
6.	Economy	96
7.	Tourism	137
8.	Population and Religion	152
9.	Art, Architecture, Fair and Festivals	156
10.	Education	187
	Bibliography	197
	Index	199

1

State at a Glance

Madhya Pradesh is a state in central India. Its capital is Bhopal, and the largest city is Indore, with Jabalpur, Gwalior, and Ujjain being the other major cities. Nicknamed the "Heart of India" due to its geographical location in India. Madhya Pradesh is the second largest Indian state by area and the fifth largest state by populationwith over 75 million residents. It borders the states of Uttar Pradesh to the northeast, Chhattisgarh to the southeast, Maharashtra to the south, Gujarat to the west, and Rajasthan to the northwest. Its total area is 308,252 km^2. Before 2000, when Chhattisgarh was a part of Madhya Pradesh, Madhya Pradesh was the largest state in India and the distance between the two furthest points inside the state, Singoli and Konta, was 1500 km. Konta is presently in Sukma district of Chattisgarh state.

The area covered by the present-day Madhya Pradesh includes the area of the ancient Avanti Mahajanapada, whose capital Ujjain(also known as Avantika) arose as a major city during the second wave of Indian urbanisation in the sixth century BCE. Subsequently, the region was ruled by the major dynasties of India. By the early 18th century, the region was divided into several small kingdoms which were captured by the British and incorporated into Central Provinces and Berar and the Central India Agency. After India's independence, Madhya Pradesh state was created with Nagpur as its capital:

this state included the southern parts of the present-day Madhya Pradesh and northeastern portion of today's Maharashtra. In 1956, this state was reorganised and its parts were combined with the states of Madhya Bharat, Vindhya Pradesh and Bhopal to form the new Madhya Pradesh state, the Marathi-speaking Vidarbha region was removed and merged with the then Bombay State. This state was the largest in India by area until 2000, when its southeastern Chhattisgarh region was made as a separate state.

Rich in mineral resources, MP has the largest reserves of diamond and copper in India. More than 30% of its area is under forest cover. Its tourism industry has seen considerable growth, with the state topping the National Tourism Awards in 2010–11. In recent years, the state's GDP growth has been above the national average.

Land: Districts

Area	: 443,446 sq. km
Capital	: Bhopal
Districts	: 45
Population	: 66,181,170
Male	: 34,232,048
Female	: 31,949,122
Literacy	: 43.45%
Language	: Hindi

A part of Madhya Pradesh has been separated and formed into a new state Chattisgarh from November 1, 2000. The details given here are before the separation. Click on Chattisgarh for more information. Madhya Pradesh situated in the centre of India, is surrounded by Maharashtra and Andhra Pradesh in the south, Uttar Pradesh and Rajasthan in the north, Bihar and Orissa in the east and Gujarat in the west. The state of Madhya Pradesh came into existence on November 1, 1956.

Except for the valleys of the Narmada and the Tapti, Madhya Pradesh consists of a plateau with a mean elevation of 1600 ft. above sea level, interspersed with the mountains of the Vindhya and the Satpura ranges. The main river systems are the Chambal, Betwa, Sindh, Narmada, Tapti, Mahanadi and Indravati. Nearly a third of the state's area is covered with tropical forests ranging between the rivers Chambal in the north and Godavari in the south. To the east of Chambal, the area has rocky surface and thick forest. Farther north, the topography of the plains stretches up to the ravines of Chambal.

The highlands of Malwa present an appearance of waving fields of grain and the green luxuriance among the shades of mango and tamarind trees clustering round the rural habitations. The inhabitants of this plateau are mostly agriculturists. The low lying area in the north of Malwa which touches the tract around Gwalior has a different appeal. Its north-east side gradually extends to *y* Bundelkhand and meets the Kaimur Hills in Baghelkhand.

Here the people are more sturdy and of lesser height as compared to the peasants of Malwa. The hilly regions fall mainly on the Vindhya and Satpura ranges where Bhils, Gonds, Korkus and other tribes of mixed descent practice agriculture. The river Narmada which rises from Amarkantak begins to run through a rocky bed near Jabalpur and Mandla. It emerges near Mandhata and widens its flow near Maheshwar in Nimad. During the rainy season a rich growth of vegetation is visible all around. The black soil of Malwa bears magnificent crops.

The climate is extreme in the north of Madhya Pradesh. It is cool and breezy in the central parts and humid in the eastern and southern regions.

Capital	
- Coordinates	Bhopal
- 23.17° N 77.21° E	
Largest city	Indore
Population (2001)	
- Density	60,385,118 (7th)
- 196/km^2	

Area	
- Districts	308,144 km² (2nd)
- 48	
Time zone	IST (UTC+5:30)
Establishment	
- Governor	
- Chief Minister	
- Legislature (seats)	1956-11-01
- Balram Jakhar	
- Shivraj Singh Chouhan	
- Unicameral (231)	
Official language(s)	Hindi
Abbreviation (ISO)	IN-MP

Madhya Pradesh: Often called the *Heart of India*, is a state in central India. Its capital is Bhopal. Madhya Pradesh was originally the largest state in India until November 1, 2000 when the state of Chhattisgarh was carved out. It borders the states Uttar Pradesh, Chhattisgarh, Maharashtra, Gujarat and Rajasthan.

The name Malwa is derived from the ancient Aryan tribe of Malavas, about whom very little is known apart from the fact that they founded the Vikrama Samvat; this is a calendar dating from 57 BC that is widely used in India and that is popularly associated with the king Chandragupta Vikramaditya. The name Malava is derived from the Sanskrit term Malav, and means "part of the abode of Lakshmi". The location of the Malwa or Moholo, mentioned by the 7th century Chinese traveller Xuanzang, is plausibly identified with present-day Gujarat. The region is cited as Malibah in Arabic records, such as Kamilu-t Tawarikh by Ibn Asir.

Ujjain, also known historically as Ujjaiyini and Avanti, emerged as the first major centre in the Malwa region during India's second wave of urbanisation in the 7th century BC (the first wave was the Indus Valley Civilization). Around 600 BC an earthen rampart was built around Ujjain, enclosing a city of considerable size. Avanti was one of the prominent mahajanapadas of the Indo-Aryans. In the post-Mahabharata period—around 500 BC—Avanti was an important kingdom in western India; it was ruled by the Haihayas, a people who were possibly of mixed Indo-Aryan and aboriginal descent, who were responsible for the destruction of Naga power in western India.

The region was conquered by the Maurya empire in the mid-4th century BC. Ashoka, who was later a Mauryan emperor, was governor of Ujjain in his youth. After the death of Ashoka in 232 BC, the Maurya Empire began to collapse.

Although evidence is sparse, Malwa was probably ruled by the Kushanas and the Shakas during the 2nd and 1st centuries BC. Ownership of the region was the subject of dispute between the Western Kshatrapas and the Satavahanas during the first three centuries AD. Ujjain emerged a major trading centre during the 1st century AD. Rani Rupmati Pavilion at Mandu, built by Miyan Bayezid Baz Bahadur (1555–62)

Malwa became part of the Gupta Empire during the reign of Chandragupta II (375–413), also known as *Vikramaditya*, who conquered the region, driving out the Western Kshatrapas. The Gupta period is widely regarded as a golden age in the history of Malwa, when Ujjain served as the empire's western capital.

Kalidasa, Aryabhata and Varahamihira were all based in Ujjain, which emerged as a major centre of learning, especially in astronomy and mathematics.

Around 500, Malwa re-emerged from the dissolving Gupta empire as a separate kingdom; in 528, Yasodharman of Malwa defeated the Hunas, who had invaded India from the north-west. During the seventh century, the region became part of Harsha's empire, and he disputed the region with the Chalukya king Pulakesin II of Badami in the Deccan. In 786 the region was captured by the Rashtrakuta kings of the Deccan, and was disputed between the Rashtrakutas and the Pratihara kings of Kannauj until the early part of the tenth century.

From the mid-tenth century, Malwa was ruled by the Paramara clan of Rajputs, who established a capital at Dhar. King Bhoj, who ruled from about 1010 to 1060, was known as the great polymath philosopher-king of medieval India; his extensive writings cover philosophy, poetry, medicine, veterinary science, phonetics, yoga, and archery. Under his rule Malwa became an intellectual centre of India. Bhoj also founded the city of Bhopal to secure the eastern part of his kingdom. His successors ruled until about 1200, when Malwa was conquered by the Delhi Sultanate.

Dilawar Khan, previously Malwa's governor under the rule of the Delhi sultanate, declared himself sultan of Malwa in 1401 after the Mongol conqueror Timur attacked Delhi, causing the break-up of the sultanate into smaller states. Khan started the *Malwa Sultanate* and established a capital at Mandu, high in the Vindhya Range overlooking the Narmada River valley. His son and successor, Hoshang Shah (1405–35), embellished Mandu.

Hoshang Shah's son, Ghazni Khan, ruled for only a year and was succeeded by Sultan Mahmud Khalji (1436–69), the first of the Khalji sultans of Malwa, who expanded the state to include parts of Gujarat, Rajasthan, and the Deccan. The Muslim sultans invited the Rajputs to settle in the country. In the early 16th century, the sultan sought the aid of the sultans of Gujarat to counter the growing power of the Rajputs, while the Rajputs sought the support of the Sesodia Rajput kings of Mewar. Gujarat stormed Mandu in 1518 and 1531, and shortly after that, the Malwa sultanate collapsed. The Mughal emperor Akbar captured Malwa in 1562 and made it a province of his empire. Mandu was abandoned by the 17th century.

HISTORY

Isolated remains of *Homo erectus* found in Hathnora in the Narmada Valley indicate that Madhya Pradesh might have been inhabited in the Middle Pleistocene era. Painted pottery dated to the later mesolithic period has been found in the

Bhimbetka rock shelters. Chalcolithic sites belonging to Kayatha culture (2100–1800 BCE) and Malwa culture (1700–1500 BCE) have been discovered in the western part of the state.

Mesolithic rock painting, Bhimbetka, a UNESCO World Heritage Site

Kandariya Mahadev, Khajuraho

Bateshwar temple complex, Padavli, Morena

Chausath Yogini Temple, Mitavli, Morena

Teli Ka Mandir, Gwalior Fort

Sahastra-bahu Temple, Gwalior Fort

Shiva Temple in Bhojpur

Lakshmi Temple, Orchha

Ancient temples, Amarkantak

Gwalior Fort, Gwalior

The city of Ujjain arose as a major centre in the region, during the second wave of Indian urbanisation in the sixth century BCE. It served as the capital of the Avanti kingdom. Other kingdoms mentioned in ancient epics—Malava, Karusha, Dasarna and Nishada—have also been identified with parts of Madhya Pradesh.

Chandragupta Maurya united northern India around 320 BCE, establishing the Mauryan Empire, which included all of modern-day Madhya Pradesh. Ashoka the greatest of Mauryan rulers brought the region under firmer control. After the decline of the Maurya empire, the region was contested among the Sakas, the Kushanas, the Satavahanas, and several local dynasties during the 1st to 3rd centuries CE. Heliodorus, the Greek Ambassador to the court of the Shunga king Bhagabhadra erected the Heliodorus pillarnear Vidisha.

Ujjain emerged as the predominant commercial centre of western India from the first century BCE, located on the trade routes between the Ganges plain and India's Arabian Sea ports. The Satavahana dynasty of the northern Deccan and the Saka dynasty of the Western Satraps fought for the control of Madhya Pradesh during the 1st to 3rd centuries CE.

The Satavahana king Gautamiputra Satakarni inflicted a crushing defeat upon the Saka rulers and conquered parts of Malwa and Gujarat in the 2nd century CE.

Subsequently, the region came under the control of the Gupta empire in the 4th and 5th centuries, and their southern neighbours, the Vakataka's. The rock-cut temples at Bagh Caves in the Kukshi tehsil of the Dhar district attest to the presence of the Gupta dynasty in the region, supported by the testimony of a Badwani inscription dated to the year of 487 CE. The attacks of the Hephthalites or White Huns brought about the collapse of the Gupta empire, which broke up into smaller states. The king Yasodharman of Malwadefeated the Huns in 528, ending their expansion. Later, Harsha (c. 590–647) ruled the northern parts of the state. Malwa was ruled by the south Indian Rashtrakuta Dynasty from the late 8th century to the 10th century. When the south Indian Emperor Govinda IIIof the Rashtrakuta dynasty annexed Malwa, he set up the family of one of his subordinates there, who took the name of Paramara.

The Medieval period saw the rise of the Rajput clans, including the Paramaras of Malwa and the Chandelas of Bundelkhand. The Chandellas built the majestic Hindu-Jain temples at Khajuraho, which represent the culmination of Hindu temple architecture in Central India. The Gurjara-Pratihara dynasty also held sway in northern and western Madhya Pradesh at this time. It also left some monuments of architectural value in Gwalior. Southern parts of Madhya Pradesh like Malwa were several times invaded by the south Indian Western Chalukya Empire which imposed its rule on the Paramara kingdom of Malwa.

The Paramara king Bhoja (c. 1010–1060) was a renowned polymath. The small Gond kingdoms emerged in the Gondwana and Mahakoshal regions of the state. Northern Madhya Pradesh was conquered by the Turkic Delhi Sultanate in the 13th century. After the collapse of the Delhi Sultanate at the end of the 14th century, independent regional kingdoms re-emerged, including the Tomara kingdom of Gwalior and the Muslim Sultanate of Malwa, with its capital at Mandu.

The Malwa Sultanate was conquered by the Sultanate of Gujarat in 1531. In the 1540s, most parts of the state fell to Sher Shah Suri, and subsequently to the Hindu king Hemu. Hemu, who had earlier served as the General of the Suri dynasty, operated from the Gwalior Fort during 1553–56 and became the ruler of Delhi as a Vikramaditya king winning 22 battles continuously from Bengal to Gujrat and defeating Akbar's forces in the Battle of Delhi on 7 October 1556.

However, he chose Delhi as his capital after his formal Coronation and left Gwalior. After Hemu's defeat by Akbar at the Second Battle of Panipat in 1556, most of Madhya Pradesh came under the Mughal rule. Gondwana and Mahakoshal remained under the control of Gond kings, who acknowledged Mughal supremacy but enjoyed virtual autonomy.

The Mughal control weakened considerably after the death of Emperor Aurangzeb in 1707.

Between 1720 and 1760, the Marathas took control of most of Madhya Pradesh, resulting in the establishment of semi-autonomous states under the nominal control of the Peshwa of Pune: the Holkars of Indoreruled much of Malwa, Puars ruled Dewas and Dhar, the Bhonsles of Nagpur dominated Mahakoshal-Gondwana area, while the Scindias of Gwalior controlled the northern parts of the state. The most notable Maratha rulers of the region were Mahadji Shinde, Ahilyabai

Holkar and Yashwantrao Holkar. Besides these, there were several other small states, including Bhopal, Orchha, and Rewa. The Bhopal state, which paid tribute to both the Marathas and the Nizam of Hyderabad, was founded by Dost Mohammed Khan, a former General in the Mughal army.

After the Third Anglo-Maratha War, the British took control of the entire region. All the sovereign states in the region became princely states of British India, governed by the Central India Agency.

The Mahakoshal region became a British province: the Saugor and Nerbudda Territories. In 1861, the British merged the Nagpur Province with the Saugor and Nerbudda Territories to form the Central Provinces.

During the 1857 uprising, rebellions happened in the northern parts of the state, led by leaders like Tatya Tope. However, these were crushed by the British and the princes loyal to them. The state witnessed a number of anti-British activities and protests during the Indian independence movement. Several notable leaders such as Chandra Shekhar Azad, B. R. Ambedkar, Shankar Dayal Sharma and Atal Bihari Vajpayee were born in what is now Madhya Pradesh.

After the independence of India, Madhya Pradesh was created in 1950 from the former British Central Provinces and Berar and the princely states of Makrai and Chhattisgarh, with Nagpur as the capital of the state. The new states of Madhya Bharat, Vindhya Pradesh, and Bhopal were formed out of the Central India Agency.

In 1956, the states of Madhya Bharat, Vindhya Pradesh, and Bhopal were merged into Madhya Pradesh, and the Marathi-speaking southern region Vidarbha, which included Nagpur, was ceded to Bombay state. Jabalpur was chosen to be the capital of the state but at the last moment, due to some political pressure, Bhopal was made the state capital. In November 2000, as part of the Madhya Pradesh Reorganization Act, the southeastern portion of the state split off to form the new state of Chhattisgarh.

SPORTS

In 2013, state govt declared Malkhamb as the state sport.

Cricket, Kabaddi, hockey, football, basketball, volleyball, cycling, swimming, badminton and table tennis are the popular sports in the state. Traditional games like kho kho, gilli danda, sitoliya, kanche and langdi are popular in the rural areas.

Snooker, a cue sport, generally regarded as having been invented in Jabalpur by British Army officers, is popular in many of the English-speaking and Commonwealth countries, with top professional players attaining multimillion-pound career earnings from the game.

Cricket is the most popular sport in Madhya Pradesh. There are three international cricket stadiums in the state – Nehru Stadium (Indore), Roop Singh Stadium (Gwalior) and Holkar Cricket Stadium (Indore). Madhya Pradesh cricket team's best performances in Ranji Trophy was in 1998–99, when the Chandrakant Pandit-led team ended as the runner-up. Its predecessor, the Indore-based Holkar cricket team, had won the Ranji Trophy four times.

Aishbagh Stadium in Bhopal is the home ground for World Series Hockey team Bhopal Badshahs. The state also has a football team that participates in the Santosh Trophy.

MP United FC is an Indian football that played in the 2nd Division I-League.

On 6 December 2017, the Madhya Pradesh Chief Minister Shivraj Singh Chouhan announced that players from the state would be given government jobs on winning medals in international events.

MADHYA PRADESH ORIGIN

The ancient Vedas record the marriage of king Dashrath of Uttar Kosal, father of Lord Rama of the epic Ramayana, with the princess of Dakshin kosal (a part of modern Madhya Pradesh). It is believed that the Lord Rama & Sita spent a major part of their 14 years exile in Chitrakoot located in the Dandaka forest area, north of the Vindhyas. Archeological explorations & excavations provide a glimpse of the ancient period from the earliest times to about the 13th century AD. The finds speak of a developed ancient civilization & reflect the glorious & chequered history of its rulers & warriors & a rich cultural past. Historically known as Malwa, Madhya Pradesh – the second largest cenrally located state in India is called the very heart of India.

Madhya Pradesh History

The history of Madhya Pradesh goes back to the time of Ashoka, the great Mauryan ruler. Major portion of Central India formed part of the Gupta Empire (300-550 AD). In the first half of the seventh century it was part of domains of famous emperor Harsha. The close of tenth century was a period of confusion. In the early eleventh century the muslims entered central India, First Mahmud of Ghazni & then Mohammad Gori who incorporated certain parts with Sultanate of Delhi. It also formed part of Mughal empire with the rise of Maratha's. Till the death of Madhoji Scindia in 1794, Marathas ruled supreme in Central India, but after that independent & smaller states came into being. The disintegrated smaller states paved way for British suzerainty. Some great women rulers like Rani Ahilyabai Holkar of Indore, Gond queen Rani Kamla devi & Rani Durgawati have carved a nick for them in history.

When India became independent in 1947, the British Indian province of Central Provinces and Berar formed Madhya Pradesh. Boundary changes followed; the state of Chhattisgarh was carved out of Madhya Pradesh.

Statehood

After Independence, all the states signed the instruments of accession in to the Indian Union & on 28th May, 1948 a new state, Madhya Bharat came into existence with Indore & Gwalior as its capital. In the north, as the result of merger of 35 princely states of Bundelkhand & Baghelkhand, Vindhya Pradesh cane into being in April 1948 & in 1952, an elected ministry was formed with Rewa as its capital.

In the North, as the result of merger of 35 princely of Bundelkhand & Baghelkhand, Vindhya Pradesh came into being in April 1948 & in 1952 an elected ministry was formed with Rewa as its capital. The state of Bhopal came into existence in June, 1949 & only in 1952 a popular ministry was formed. The state of Madhya Pradesh formed on 1st November 1956 was a conglomeration of Mahakosal, Madhya Bharat, Vindhya Pradesh, Bhopal state & Seronj sub division of the Kota District of Rajasthan. On 1st November 2001 Chhatisgarh was carved out of Madhya Pradesh. At present comprises of 45 district which are further subdivided into 264 tehsils & is the second largest state in India.

Tourism

Madhya Pradesh, as its name implies, lies in the heart of India, whose topography ranges from plateau with the Vindhya & the Satpura mountain ranges, the plains in the east, meandering rivers, rocky hills & ravines to lush green forests. State offers all important pillars of Indian tourism like pilgrim tourism, wildlife tourism, heritage tourism, buddhism, adventure sports etc.

The state boasts of a wide variety of attractions to suit all tourist tastes, from ancient temples to national parks & sanctuaries, stupas, forts & palaces, a host of cultural & tourist festivals to splendid venues for international conference & conventions of global standards.

The best known tourism products of Madhya Pradesh in global & national tourism market are its heritage & archeological sites, wildlife territories, pilgrimage centres, leisure & business centres & the rich classical, folk & tribal culture. The principal destinations are Khajuraho, Kanha, Sanchi, Mandu, Gwalior – Shivpuri, Pachmarhi, Bandhavgarh, Satpura National Park, Pench, Amarkantak, Ujjain, Omkareshwar, Bhedaghat, Orchha & Chitrakoot & the dynamic business centres of Bhopal & Indore.

Madhya Pradesh State Tourism Development Corporation Ltd. (MPSTDC), a state government organization is the nodal agency responsible for development & promotion to attract tourists to this very heart of India.

Fairs & Festivals

The province of Madhya Pradesh is the milieu of fairs and festivals, which also becomes its style mantra. In other words, culture of Madhya Pradesh is nurtured due to exquisite festival celebrations. Apart from celebrating all other Indian festivals like Holi, Dusshera, the tribal festivals and fairs are also observed in full vigor and merrymaking. Revelry, drinks and alien amusement like cock fighting, dancing label these tribal festivals in Madhya Pradesh. 'Kalidas Samaroh', 'Tansen Samaroh' and a dance fete in Khajuraho are celebrated, in great fiesta, with vast number of avid participants. Religious festivals too are observed with veneration. In West Nimar and Jabua regions of Mandhyanchal , a colorful festival called Bhagoria Haat is feted by the Bhils and Bhilalas tribes. It is a mass 'swayamvara', is held in vividness before Holi festival in the month of March

People

The population of Madhya Pradesh is about 60.38 Millions (2001 census), an increase of 24.34% & the population density is 196 people per square kilometer. More than 75% of state population resides in villages whose main occupation is agriculture, while the rest of the population lives in towns. Indore district is the most populated one. Number of females per thousand male (sex ratio) in the state is 919 where as the literacy rate is 63.70%. The majority population is Hindu with Muslims making up the largest minority community.

The life style, culture & customs of this community mostly resemble the Hindu religion though they still strongly believe in orthodox traditions. Gond is the best known tribe & forms the largest group in Madhya Pradesh. Bhils, the second largest tribe are largely concentrated in the area around Jhabua, Khargone, Dhar & Ratlam. Baigas believe themselves to be descendants of Dravid & this backward tribe is found in Mandla, balaghat, Shahdol & Sidhi District. Bharia tribe has major concentration in Jabalpur & Chhindwara district of Madhya Pradesh.Korku tribal community is administered by the head of a panchayat (called Sarpanch) & they are found in Hoshangabad, Betul, Chhindwara, Harda & Khandwa districts of Madhya Pradesh. Santia is a tribe of Malwawho believe themselves to be originally a martial Rajput tribe. Lesser known tribe like Dhanuk, Panika, Saur still form an important group.

Language

Hindi, the official language of Madhya Pradesh is the most widely spoken language. It is the predominant language of the official work. It is not very difficult for locals even in remote corners to understand Hindi. It is widely spoken by sizeable numbers engaged in the hospitality & service industry.

One would see words of English & Hindi both used on signages, milestones, shop & office signboards. The language Marathi is also widespread. Malwi, Bundeli, bagheli, Nimari are the commonly spoken regional languages. The dilects like, Gondi, Bhilli is the most common spoken language among the tribal community of gond & Bhils respectively. Chhatisgarh is spoken by majority in the east & southeast region of the Madhya Pradesh.

Climate

Madhya Pradesh has a subtropical climate. Like most of north India it has a hot dry summer(April-June) followed by monsoon rains (July-September) and a cool and relatively dry winter. The average rainfall is about 1,370 mm (53.9 in). It decreases from east to west. The south-eastern districts have the heaviest rainfall, some places receiving as much as 2,150 mm (84.6 in), while the western and north-western districts receive 1,000 mm (39.4 in) or less.

AFTER INDIAN INDEPENDENCE

Madhya Pradesh was created in 1950 from the former British Central Provinces and Berar and the princely states of

Makrai and Chhattisgarh, with Nagpur as the capital of the state. The new states of Madhya Bharat, Vindhya Pradesh, and Bhopal were formed out of the Central India Agency. In 1956, the states of Madhya Bharat, Vindhya Pradesh, and Bhopal were merged into Madhya Pradesh, and the Marathi-speaking southern region Vidarbha, which included Nagpur, was ceded to Bombay state.

Bhopal became the new capital of the state. In November 2000, as part of the Madhya Pradesh Reorganization Act, the southeastern portion of the state split off to form the new state of Chhattisgarh.

2

Culture and Society

CULTURE

Bagh Print Traditional hand block print craft in Bagh

A man playing flute in Orchha, with a white tilak on his forehead, and holy saffron-coloured clothes.

Sand sculpture by Sudarshan Pattnaik at Bandrabhan near Hoshangabad

Four sites in Madhya Pradesh have been declared World Heritage Sites by UNESCO: the Khajuraho Group of Monuments (1986) including Devi Jagadambi temple, Khajuraho, Buddhist Monuments at Sanchi (1989) and the Rock Shelters of Bhimbetka (2003). Other architecturally significant or scenic sites include Ajaigarh, Amarkantak, Asirgarh, Bandhavgarh, Bawangaja, Bhopal, Vidisha, Chanderi, Chitrakuta, Dhar, Gwalior, Indore, Nemavar, Jabalpur, Burhanpur, Maheshwar, Mandleshwar, Mandu, Omkareshwar, Orchha, Pachmarhi, Shivpuri, Sonagiri, Mandla and Ujjain.

Madhya Pradesh is noted for its classical and folk music. Some of the noted Hindustani classical music gharanas in Madhya Pradesh include the Maihar gharana, the Gwalior gharana and Senia gharana. Two of the medieval India's most noted singers, Tansen and Baiju Bawra, were born near Gwalior in present-day Madhya Pradesh. Noted Dhrupad exponents Aminuddin Dagar (Indore), Gundecha Brothers (Ujjain) and Uday Bhawalkar (Ujjain) were also born in present-day Madhya Pradesh. The birthplaces of noted playback singers Kishore Kumar (Khandwa) and Lata Mangeshkar (Indore) and singer and composer Aadesh Shrivastava (Jabalpur) are also located in MP. The local styles of folk singing include Faga, Bhartahari, Sanja geet, Bhopa, Kalbelia, Bhat/Bhand/Charan, Vasdeva, Videsia, Kalgi Turra, Nirgunia, Alha, Pandwani Gayan and Garba Garbi Govalan.

The major folk dances of MP are Rai, Karma, Saila, Matki, Gangaur, Badhai, Baredi, Naurata, Ahiri and Bhagoria.

A Maratha-styled Sculpture from Maheshwar: The culture of Malwa has been significantly influenced by Gujarati and Rajasthani culture, because of their geographic proximity. Marathi influence is also visible, because Malwa was the recent rule by the Marathas. The main language of Malwa is *Malvi*, although Hindi is widely spoken in the cities. This Indo-European language is subclassified as Indo-Aryan.

The language is sometimes referred to as Malavi or Ujjaini. Malvi is part of the Rajasthani branch of languages; *Nimadi* is spoken in the Nimar region of Madhya Pradesh and in Rajasthan. The dialects of Malvi are, in alphabetical order, *Bachadi*, *Bhoyari*, *Dholewari*, *Hoshangabadi*, *Jamral*, *Katiyai*, Malvi Proper, *Patvi*, *Rangari*, *Rangri* and *Sondwari*. A survey in 2001 found only four dialects: Ujjaini (in the districts of Ujjain, Indore, Dewas and Sehore), *Rajawari* (Ratlam, Mandsaur and Neemuch), *Umadwari* (Rajgarh) and *Sondhwari* (Jhalawar, in Rajasthan). About 55% of the population of Malwa can converse in and about 40% of the population is literate in Hindi, the official language of the Madhya Pradesh state.

Traditional Malwa food has elements of both Gujarati and Rajasthani cuisine. Traditionally, jowar was the staple cereal, but after the green revolution in India, wheat has replaced jowar as the most important food crop; many are vegetarians. Since the climate is mostly dry throughout the year, most people rely on stored foods such as pulses, and green vegetables are rare. A typical snack of Malwa is the *bhutta ri kees* (made with grated corn roasted in ghee and later cooked in milk with spices). *Chakki ri shaak* is made of wheat dough, which is washed under running water, steamed and then used in a gravy of curd.

The traditional bread of Malwa is called *baati/bafla*, which is essentially a small, round ball of wheat flour, roasted over dung cakes, in the traditional way. *Baati* is typically eaten with dal (pulses), while *baflas* are dripping with ghee and soaked with dal. The *amli ri kadhi* is *kadhi* made with tamarind instead of yogurt. Sweet cakes, made of a variety of wheat called *tapu*, are prepared during religious festivities. Sweet cereal called *thulli* is also typically eaten with milk or yoghurt. Traditional desserts include *mawa-bati* (milk-based sweet similar to Gulab jamun), *khoprapak* (coconut-based sweet), *shreekhand* (yogurt based) and *malpua*.

Lavani is a widely practised form of folk music in southern Malwa, which came through the Marathas. The *Nirguni Lavani* (philosophical) and the *Shringari Lavani* (erotic) are the two of the main genres. The Bhils have their own folk songs, which are always accompanied by dance.

The folk musical modes of Malwa are of four or five notes, and in rare cases six. The devotional music of the *Nirguni* cult is popular throughout Malwa. Legends of *Raja* Bhoj and *Bijori*, the *Kanjar* girl, and the tale of *Balabau* are popular themes for folk songs. Insertions known as *stobha* are commonly used in Malwa music; this can occur in four ways: the *matra stobha* (syllable insertion), *varna stobha* (letter insertion), *shabda stobha* (word insertion) and *vakya stobha* (sentence insertion).

Typical Countryside Near Mhow during the Monsoon Season

Malwa was the centre of Sanskrit literature during and after the Gupta period. The region's most famous playwright, Kalidasa, is considered to be the greatest Indian writer ever. His first surviving play is *Malavikagnimitra* (Malavika and Agnimitra). Kalidasa's second play, his masterpiece, is the Abhijnanauakuntalam, which tells the story of king Dushyanta, who falls in love with a girl of lowly birth, the lovely Shakuntala. The last of Kalidasa's surviving plays is *Vikramuurvashiiya* ("Urvashi conquered by valour"). Kalidasa also wrote the epic poems *Raghuvamsha* ("Dynasty of Raghu"), *Ritusamhara* and *Kumarasambhava* ("Birth of the war god"), as well as the lyric *Meghaduuta* ("The cloud messenger").

Swang is a popular dance form in Malwa; its roots go back to the origins of the Indian theatre tradition in the first millennium BC. Since women did not participate in the dance-drama form, men enacted their roles. *Swang* incorporates suitable theatrics and mimicry, accompanied alternatately by song and dialogue. The genre is dialogue-oriented rather than movement-oriented.

Mandana (literally painting) wall and floor paintings are the best-known painting traditions of Malwa. White drawings stand out in contrast to the base material consisting of a mixture of red clay and cow dung. Peacocks, cats, lions, goojari, bawari, the swastika and chowk are some motifs of this style. *Sanjhya* is a ritual wall painting done by young girls during the annual period when Hindus remember and offer ritual oblation to their ancestors. Malwa miniature paintings are well known for their intricate brushwork.

In the 17th century, an offshoot of the Rajasthani school of miniature painting, known as *Malwa painting*, was centred largely in Malwa and Bundelkhand. The school has preserved the style of the earliest examples, such as the *Rasikapriya* series dated 1636 (after a poem analysing the love sentiment) and the *Amaru Sataka* (a 17th-century Sanskrit poem). The paintings from this school are flat compositions on black and chocolate-brown backgrounds, with figures shown against a solid colour patch, and architecture painted in vibrant colours.

Women Making Offerings on the Banks of the River Shipra, Ujjain

The biggest festival of Malwa is the *Simhastha mela*, held every 12 years, in which more than a million pilgrims take a holy dip in river Shipra. The festival of *Gana-gour* is celebrated in honour of Shiva and Parvati. The history of the festival goes back to *Rano Bai*, whose parental home was in Malwa, but who was married in Rajasthan. Rano Bai was strongly attached to Malwa, and did not want to stay in Rajasthan. After marriage, she was allowed to visit Malwa only once a year; *Gana-gour* symbolises these annual return visits. The festival is observed by the women in the region once in the month of *Chaitra* (mid-March) and *Bhadra* (mid-August).

The *Ghadlya* (earthen pot) festival is celebrated by the girls of the region, who gather to visit every house in their village in the evenings, carrying earthen pots with holes for the light from oil lamps inside to escape. In front of every house, the girls recite songs connected with the Ghadlya and receive food or money in return. The *Gordhan* festival is celebrated on the 16th day in the month of Kartika. The Bhils of the region sing *Heeda* anectodal songs to the cattle, while the women sing the *Chandrawali* song, associated with Krishna's romance.

The most popular fairs are held in the months of *Phalguna*, *Chaitra*, *Bhadra*, *Ashvin* and *Kartik*. The *Chaitra* fair, held at

Biaora, and the *Gal yatras*, held at more than two dozen villages in Malwa are remarkable. Many fairs are held in the tenth day of the month of *Bhadra* to mark the birth of Tejaji. The *Triveni mela* is held at Ratlam, and other fairs take place in *Kartika* at Ujjain, Mandhata (Nimad), Nayagaon, among others. In the Belisarius series, by David Drake and Eric Flint, the people of Malwa are chosen by malicious beings from the future to change the course of history. The Byzantine general Belisarius is set against them by a creature sent by a benevolent group of future beings.

CUSTOMS AND TRADITIONS

The Socio-Religious system of any region usually brings the members of different castes and creeds closer to having interdependent relationships. Common experiences are shared by them, permitting each other to regulate their ritual practices. The fundamental structure of the social organisation in Madhya Pradesh is particularly caste-based. Despite the cultural diversity, the state presents an interesting account of Adivasi and non-Adivasi customs and traditions.

THE GHOTUL

The unique institution of the Ghotul is for the unmarried boys and girls of the Muria tribe. As a village dormitory, the Ghotul is traditionally sanctioned by the tribal customs. The Ghotul is a large hut or a group of huts with a compound around where the Muria youngsters assemble after sunset. It is a centre of social and emotional activities which also helps the Muria boys and girls of Baster to group up in a sort of group discipline.

The institution of Ghotul plays an important part in shaping the life of the Muria Adivasis. It deepens the sense of social democracy and leads the members above jealousy and possessiveness. Individualism has no place in Ghotul. The institution serves as a most preventive measures of crime, for the boys and girls learn in the Ghotul to share everything and scorn acquisitiveness.

In the Ghotul, the boy members are known as Chelik and the girl members as Motiari. The relation between Chelik and Motiari are governed by the type of the Ghotul to which they belong. In the older classical type of Ghotul, boys and girls pair off in a more or less permanent relationship which lasts till marriage. In the modern form of Ghotul, such exclusive associations are forbidden and partners must constantly be changed.

In the Ghotul, friendliness, sympathy, and unity are of prime importance. Love finds the right place as it unifies the members of the tribe and keeps them in good mood without the slightest tinge of possessiveness.

The Ghotul evening begins with chats and laughter of the boys and girls. One of the important routines of the Ghotul is saluting one another in a monotonous rhythmic way known as johar, in which each person greets the other by the name, individually. Another interesting custom practiced by the Muria Ghotul is the form of conventional enquiries made by the leading boy. But this is a routine affair.

Any time after sunset the male members begin to arrive at the Ghotul with their belongings such as sleeping mats, tobacco-pouches or other such things they might need at night. Few of the boys gather round the fire or scatter about the compound or else lie down under the thatched roof of the open huts and puff their chongis, the country cigarettes. A couple of them get busy with their musical instruments. Soon the girls follow and the atmosphere of the Ghotul brightens up. Girls seem more enthusiastic to have the music and dance. A dance song called Rela gets the favour of the gathering.

After an hour or two the boys and girls like to squat round the fire and it seems story-telling becomes a favourite pastime. At this hour the boys and girls join together freely. At fairly late night, Belosa, the leader of the girls and Sirdar, the leader of the boys decide how the couples shall be paired. The decision comes as a romance mixed with duty and charm, get equal chances in this democracy of romance.

Dress: The peasant population of the state wears the dhoti. A white or a black jacket called bandi or mirzai is still in vogue in Bundelkhand and Malwa. Safa is worn on the head in the eastern parts of the state and pagri or paga (turban) is preferred in the western regions. Among the new generations trousers, socks and shirts have become very common. Women wear coloured lehnga and choli.

A piece of cloth known as orni or lugra is used to cover the head and the shoulders. In the central region they prefer red and black colours, while yellow, blue and green are admired by the Chhathsgarhi women. Kanchali is stitched out of coloured pieces of cloth. It is a sort of bodice used for covering the breasts only by tying it at the back with strings, called Kasana in the Malwi dialect.

Marriage: Marriage is conceived as a sanskar wherein an individual is made to perform an important task of perpetualising his patriline. By attaining marital status he fulfils the essential which Manu has recommended.

Marriage within an endogamous group is performed with a view to keep racial party. Violation of this rule often results into excommunication in many castes living in villages. Exogamy is permitted but it is always a complicated matter to find out a match outside one's own kin group. A village is usually treated as an exogamous unit from where girls may be selected.

Among the same gotra, marriage is not strictly prohibited in the agricultural communities of central Madhya Pradesh. The gotra is understood to be a wider link that a clan maintains. Within the same link there is always another close link of gotra in which marriage relation is not permissible. Two brothers could marry two sisters or giving and taking could be done by mutual arrangement, by a brother and sister marrying a pair of sibling.

The orthodox section of the Hindu communities follows the Vedic system. Among the enlightened section the marriage is arranged either by willing couples or by their elders. Marriage by elopement is still prevalent in the Bhils of the Vindhyas, but it is confirmed only after the bride-price is ceremonially paid off. Members of the same sect and totem are not allowed to marry.

The Raj Gonds have adopted the Hindu ceremonial. In Bastar and Chanda the primitive form of marriage is still in vogue, though the procedure is now merely symbolical. The most distinctive feature of a Gond wedding is that the procession usually starts from the bride's house and the ceremony is performed at that of the bridegroom. When a Gond wishes to marry his children he first looks to his sisters children, when he considers himself entitled to demand for his own, such a marriage being called 'bringing back the milk'.

Marriage and cohabitation together are rare except among some animistic tribes. Premarital relations are possible within certain tribal groups like the Muria and that too in their Ghotul premises. But when the relations reach to assume marital position, the wedding ceremony becomes absolutely necessary through their elders. In the Abujhmar the boy's parent visit the parents of the girl and present a pot of mahua liquor. If the pot is accepted and all other things are agreeably settled the boy and girl are declared betrothed. Paithu or Paisa Mundi is a type of marriage in which a girl goes of her own to her lover's house to live with him. Kytiyari form is an extension of cross-cousin marriage. This Muria form may be compared with the dudh lotana (bringing back the milk) form of the Gonds.

The actual marriage ceremony ranges from the most lengthy and elaborate practices to very simple ones, but the essential rites are the same. Use of turmeric and oil and the perambulation of the sacred fire or the pole and all such rituals emphasize the unity of the couple. The feast depends primarily on the availability of funds and secondarily on the customs and traditions of the respective groups.

Among the Korkens tribe of Madhya Pradesh, the father of the girl catches hold of a capable boy and brings him home. He is called Lamsena. If the Lamsena likes the girl, he has to fulfill two conditions. Firstly, he has to serve as a household servant for 6-12 months, then he has to prove that he has the capacity of a grown man (manhood). To prove his manhood, he has full liberty to have intercourse with the girl, but if the girl does not become pregnant within one year, then Lamsena is made to flee and a new one is caught instead.

There is another tradition among the Korkens, where the girl gets into the house of her fiance. If the boy agrees to marry, the marriage is settled. Otherwise the boy has to leave his house and the village/tribe and whole of his property becomes that of the girl. A similar tradition is that the father of the girl sends the daughter away to search for a life companion. Among some Korkens, the father of the girl selects a boy himself. After getting a suitable boy, the terms of payment are settled and the father of the boy takes away the bride.

SCULPTURE OF A HOLKAR COURTIER FROM FORT AHILYA

As the Mughal state weakened after 1700, the Marathas raided Malwa. Malhar Rao Holkar (1694–1766) became leader of Maratha armies in Malwa in 1724, and in 1733 the Maratha Peshwa granted him control of most of the region, which was formally ceded by the Mughals in 1738.

Another Maratha general, Anand Rao Panwar, established himself as the raja of Dhar in 1742, and the two Panwar brothers became rajas of Dewas. At the end of the 18th century, Malwa became the venue of fighting between the rival Maratha powers and the headquarters of the Pindaris, who were irregular plunderers. The Pindaris were rooted out in a campaign by the British general Lord Hastings, and further order was established under Sir John Malcolm. The Holkar dynasty ruled Malwa from Indore and Maheshwar on the Narmada until 1818, when the Marathas were defeated by the British in the Third Anglo-Maratha War, and the Holkars of Indore became a princely state of the British Raj.

After 1818 the British organised the numerous princely states of central India into the Central India Agency; the Malwa Agency was a division of Central India, with an area of 23,100 km^2

(8,919 square miles) and a population of 1,054,753 in 1901. It comprised the states of Dewas (senior and junior branch), Jaora, Ratlam, Sitamau and Sailana, together with a large part of Gwalior, parts of Indore and Tonk, and about 35 small estates and holdings. Political power was exercised from Neemuch. Upon Indian independence in 1947, the Holkars and other princely rulers acceded to India, and most of Malwa became part of the new state of Madhya Bharat, which was merged into Madhya Pradesh in 1956.

CRAFTSMANSHIP AND BELL WORK

The exquisite taste for making handicrafts is an important trait of the tribals of Madhya Pradesh.The Murias and the Marias of Bastar are excellent wood carvers. They show their art either on visible logs of wood pieces used in their dwelling hutments or on various objects of daily use.

Tobacco containers of the Murias will attract anyone for their tortoise and the sun-moon motifs and designs. Craftsmanship of the Murias can be seen in wooden blocks made for supporting hair and in wooden pins used to adorn hairdo's by the Ghotul girls. The most charming work of this tribe is the making of combs. On many of the combs leopard and other kinds of animal motifs are made. Wooden spears and utensils are intensely carved.

In Bastar those who can afford would care to erect funerary pillars in the memory of their deceased relatives. The Murias and Marias call these pillars Munde or Khamba. They are mostly made of saja or saria wood and are carved on all sides. It bears all sorts of figures.

In Bastar and other places, at the Nawa festival, the potters make toy grindstones, bullocks, horses, earthen wheels to be attached to little carts, cooking pots and tiny heaths. Murias and the Savaras make more elaborate toys which are used during their festal dances. To a long bamboo pole they attach a number of wooden animals like monkeys or lizards and arrangement of strings move them up and down so that they appear to be climbing.

Brass work occupies an important place in the craftsmanship of the Bastar tribes. The urge for creativeness reflects in most of the images made of the brass and bell metal. For preparing these figures they follow the ancient cire-perdue process. First the earthen core is made, then wax is shaped on the object which is ultimately replaced by molten metal.

TATTOOING

Tattooing is widely practiced among the Adivasis of Madhya Pradesh. They treat the tattoo marks as worthy of social importance. The Chirlya (bird) mark must be borne by a Bhil woman prior to her marriage and is always tattooed at the side angles of the eyes.

Tattooing after marriage is not regarded as auspicious. Both for the tribals and non-tribals of the peasant class the desire to attain status in their respective communities is an anthropomorphic concern. Tattooing serves as an expression to derive satisfaction through the symbolic confirmation of their group codes.

Every member tries to be with the group. Tattooing gives him a feeling of security. There is a belief among the Bhils that the figures drawn on the body are the evidence of good deeds which go with a person to his post-mortem existence. With them he is in a position to explain his past. The Bhils are more fond of their own traditional marks. From the tattoo marks, one could distinguish whether the symbols represented belong to any tribal group or any other community.

Women are used to thick tattooing on visible parts of their bodies. In the Bundelkhand region amongst the rural people there is a saying that whereas all other ornaments of a woman are taken off when she dies, tattoo marks are her only fortune she carries to the next world. Chhattisgarhi women are more fond of tattooing. They fix up the marks by injecting vegetable dye into the skin through continuous pricking of a needle point.

Tattooing is mostly done by mutual help. Godharin or the

wife of a village sorcerer is usually invited to do this job. The Dewar community of Chhattisgarh has adopted this profession as a side job. The Badnin, *i.e.* a woman of the Badna caste among the Gonds does this kind of work for token payment. She also prepares the mixture used as ink.

The practice of tattooing with the paste, prepared by lamp-black mixed with linseed oil is slowly vanishing as the professional tattooers are always available who do it by mechanical means. Tattoo marks have a great significance for the tribes of Bastar and the Bhils of Malwa and Nimad. Their tattoo figures express the kind of behaviouristic mode of their clan-complexions. The figures also represent the fineness and the symbolic beauty of the things associated with their daily life.

Painting the body on ceremonial occasions continues to be a ritual for the tribals. A male dancer always takes care to decorate his body with white and red stripes to give the impression of a tiger. The Muria dancer prefers to paints the rows of dots to look like a panther.

FOLK MUSIC

The folk musical material of the state may be classified into three groups. The first being the tribal music, which is undoubtedly very rich in content. The second group is of the countryside music. It includes legendry narratives, ceremonial songs, work songs and the songs linked with rituals, love longings and occupations. Its music survives in cross-cultural traits of social relationships.

Its structural shades vary from caste to caste and from region to region. The third group of songs has a close affinity with the Bhakti cult of the medieval period. The vast concourse of these songs draws themes from mythology and ranges from the traditional Harikatha to the simple rendering of old Bhajans, art songs, lyrics of poets Chandra Sakhi and Sukhai and the devotional songs attributed to Ramdev, etc. Thousands of songs and Vaishnav padas are sung into varied complexion under religious and devotional fervour. Some of the complexions even admit embellishment and to a small degree tanas and alap in their stylized crudeness.

The folk musical map of Madhya Pradesh has certain predominant features. The people seldom confine themselves to their own songs except when singing ritualistic songs and the one's related to wedding ceremonies. The peasant class has no taboo to sing popular songs of other racial groups. Singing up participation is instinctive and unavoidable.

The folk music of Madhya Pradesh comes from the tribal areas. Bastar which is the land of the famous Muria and Sing Maria tribes is known for its haunting melodies. The Relo is a remarkable type of the Muria song. Every young man must respond to its call. It is an everlasting favourite song of the Muria boys and girls. They may sing the Relo on any occasion.

The music of the Hill Marias and the Bhils is full of short scales. Gooning is not rare in the music of the Abujhmar tribe. The Murias of north Bastar generally sing with a high-pitched voice using five to six notes. The music and dance are interdependent among these tribes. The Murias, the Sing Marias, the Bhils and the Korkus do not share the common traits of their traditional music with the exception that the Gonds seem to have certain common layers overlapping with the Murias. They have melodies of short ambit with occasional move to the octave.

In the surrounding villages of Jagdalpur, the **Leja song** has a significant place. The Leja has its origin with the 'send off ' ritual to some dear one. Literally, the Leja means 'take it'. Many of the Leja songs are lengthy. The rhyming line serves as a relic and could be recited to unfold any song. The recitative line seldom has any affinity with the actual song. It merely helps to enhance the form of the song. Any subject could be the theme of the Leja songs. The Bhatra and the Panka classes of the Adivasi population sing numerous Leja songs.

The land of Bastar is known for the **Chait Parah and the Dhankul songs**. The former is of the seasonal category while the latter is associated with the invocation to the goddess Danteshwari.

The stock of the traditional music of Chattisgarh is semi tribal in texture. It has many traces of tribal phrases woven into the fabric of its own music. The music of Chhattisgarh is not fully agricultural in its socio-perspective.

The **marriage songs** of the Kamars are generally short. Many of them are addressed to the trumpeter Moharia. The Dadaria of this region has a pattern of rhyming lines. They are also called Ban-Bhajans or Salho. The Dadaria has a style of question-answer rendering.

The basic structure of the songs from Bundelkhand rests on the medieval sentiments. The musical compositions of the songs are simple and rigid. They have a few dominant characteristics of rhyming phrases.

The Bundelkhand region and Baghelkhand which is the land of the Baghelas are known for their heroic deeds. Hardaul is the popular deity of both these areas. Though semi-historical in character, Lala Hardaul has received deep reverence in the contents of the folk music of Bundelkhand.

The songs of the poet Isuri came into prominence among the people of this region. His four-lined compositions (Chaukaria Phag) have become part and parcel of the folk musical tradition of the region stretching down to Bhopal. In Nimad, songs attributed to Singa and Daluji are very much alive. The ballads about Chhatrasal and the Rani of Jhansi have also become one with the existing folk music. As compared to the seasonal songs and the children's songs the music of Bundelkhand is not of much antiquity.

There are romantic **Led and the Pai songs**. The Pai is associated with the Saira dance of the rainy season. The Bambulia of Bundelkhand has religious fervour and is always sung by the people who go for ceremonial bath to distant rivers. The song corresponds to the Batgamni of Mithila. The Alha of Jagnik narrates the account of fifty-two battles fought by both Alha and Udal against Prithviraj of Delhi. The Alha reciters are known as Alhets. The dirges of Nimad are full of pathos and the Sati songs of Malwa are haunted by sadness while the Jogiras and the songs about Raja Bharthari and the folk devotional type of Sakhis of Kabir, sing of the transient nature of the world. The Garbi of the Narmada valley has a softer melody than the Garba songs of Nimad. It has three variations like the Rewari Garbi, the simple Garbi and the Gujarati Garbi.

The **Lavani** came to Malwa along with the Marathas in the beginning of the eighteenth century. The Nirguni Lavani (philosophical) and the Shringari Lavani (erotic) are the two types which is popular in the south of Nimad. The Panwaras are very close to the rural population. They are sung in a quick tempo. The purity of the original tunes of folk music is mostly preserved in the ritualistic and ceremonial songs of the countryside women. The songs of the folk poet Sukhai of the Chambal ravines of Bhind and Morena districts are full of verve. The land adjoining the Braj-speaking zone is rich in love songs. The impact of Braj music is obvious on the people of Gwalior.

A large portion of Malwa and Nimad is inhabited by the Adivasis. The **songs of the Bhils**, which accompany their dances and the songs of their festivals and nuptial ceremonies give a glimpse of the life-pattern they hold. These songs are sung at an even tempo with regular rise and fall. In most of the songs, meaningless chants are introduced to fill up the gaps between the lines. The Bhils always sing in groups. Dancing is inseparable from their music. The only exception is the Dhak song which is sung with a belief to cure the physical and mental ailments of a diseased person. They treat this song as very sacred since the music of the Dhak is supposed to have a magical effect on them. In Bundelkhand, such songs are sung before Karas Dev, the village deity, whose associated songs are called Goten. The Banjara songs like the Shri Maharaj ri Bel and the Rasturavan; the long narrative, Heeda of the Gujars and Ahirs; and the Ekadasi, the Chain Singh and other ballads popular in Malwa have sustaining music.

The music of the folk-drama called Maanch has a texture of its own. The beauty of the Maanch, often reveals in its musical dialogues, recited to the accompaniment of drums.

The **folk musical modes** of Malwa are very much suited to different occasions. They depend on four to five notes. In rare cases, six notes are employed. The music of the songs sung at the time of sacrifice or rituals in remote villages gives rise to an awe, while tunes of the Jhoola songs clearly convey the swinging motion. The notes of the raga Bhoop are evidently felt in the Garbi songs of Nimad. All the song types have certain swara-scale.

In Malwa, legends about Raja Bhoj and Bijori, the Kanjar girl and the tale of Balabau have a peculiar appeal. The devotional music of the Nirguni cult is popular all over the zone. Love songs like the Naik Banjara and the Ranubai, have soft music. The agricultural society-born music has a tendency of insertion known in the musical term as 'Stobha'. This tendency is unfolded in four ways: in Matra stobha, the syllable insertion; in Varna stobha, the letter insertion; in Shabda stobha, the word insertion and in Vakya stobha, the sentence insertion. The music of Madhya Pradesh is not an exception to this mode.

FOLK DANCE

Muria Dances: The Murias of North Bastar are trained in the Ghotul for all types of their community dances. Before any dance is commenced at a wedding or a festive occasion, the Murias first worship their drums. Very often they begin with an invocation to 'Lingo Pen', the phallic deity of the tribe and the founder of the Ghotul institution. To a Muria, Lingo Pen was the first musician who taught the art of drumming to the tribal boys.

The dancing site is chosen near the Ghotul compound. On marriage celebrations, the Muria boys and girls perform a dance called Har Endanna. The dance commences with a group of boys carrying ritualistic offerings and gifts and conducting the bridegroom to the ceremonial place. In this light and happy dance, there are a variety of movements with the boy and the girl dancers and drummers participating to move in patterns with running steps and circles then changing directions, kneeling, bending and jumping. The movements of the drummers as they dance and manipulate their drums is fascinating.

Their Hulki is the loveliest of all the dances. The Karsana is performed for sheer fun and enjoyment. Both the dance-forms are quick and rich with many rhythmic nuances. In the Hulki, boys move in a ring while the girls tread way through them.

These forms are more favourite with the performing groups when they go to another village to attend wedding celebrations or else visit some fair. Their Pus Kolang expedition occurs in the month of February. During hot weather the boys and the girls meet in Chhat-Dadar expedition. Many of the dances associated to these visits are stick-dances.

Gaur Dance: The most popular among the Madhya Pradesh dances, is the Gaur dance of the Sing Marias or Tallaguda Marias (bison-horn Marias) of South Bastar. This spectacular dance symbolizes the hunting spirit of the tribe. The word 'Gaur' means a ferocious bison. The invitation for a dance is given by sounding a bamboo trumpet or a horn. Wearing head-dresses frilled with stringed 'cowries' and plumes of peacock feathers fastened to them the men folk with flutes and drums make their way to the dancing ground. Women adorned with brass fillets and bead necklaces over their tattooed bodies soon join the assemblage.

They carry dancing sticks called Tirududi in their right hands and tap them to conform with the drum-beats. They dance in their own groups by the side of the male members. But they also take the liberty to cross and re-cross in between the groups of male dancers and drummers. Their jingling anklets correspond to the songs of their lips as they move. The men beat the drums, tossing the horns and feathers of their head-gears to the rising tempo that gives the dance a wilder touch.

The men with drums usually move in a circle and create a variety of dancing patterns when they are spirited. In the bison dance (Gaur) they attack one another and chase the female dancers. The Marias imitate a number of bison movements. Most of them perform like frisky bulls, hurling wisps of grass into air, charging and tossing horns.

Saila Dance: Young boys of the plains of Chhattisgarh bring life to the post-harvest time by the Saila dance. Saila is a stick-dance and is popular among the people of Sarguja, Chhindwara and Baitul districts. But in these places, Saila is known by Danda Nach or Dandar Pate. The Saila often comes out with many variations and much buffoonery. Sometimes the dancers form a circle, each standing on one leg and supporting himself by holding on to the man in front. Then they all hop together round and round. Sometimes they pair off, or go round in a single or double line, occasionally, climbing on each other's back. The climax of a day's Saila, is the great Snake Dance. The Saila songs, of which the refrain is the monotonous Nanare nana are usually of a progressive character leading to a highly vulgar conclusion.

Saila comprises over half a dozen varieties. Some of them are named as the Baithiki Saila, the Artari Saila, the Thadi Saila, the Chamka Kunda Saila, the Chakramar Saila (lizard's dance) and the Shikari Saila. Each variation has a certain theme and distinctive feature of its own. Saila's simple form is the Dasera dance which is always performed by the Baigas before Diwali. Some of the post-harvest dances reach the climax towards the festivities of Diwali. The Diwali dances of the Ahirs and Rawats of Bilaspur and Raipur districts of the state have enough of vital appeal. Wearing tight-fitting shirts, studded with ghungrus or tiny bells and armlets of ghungurs, the Ahir dancers vigorously perform the Danda dance.

Karma Dance: Among the Gonds and the Baigas of Chhattisgarh and the Oraons of the north-west fringes of Madhya Pradesh, the Karma dance is very common. This form is associated with the fertility cult and essentially related to the Karma festival that falls in the month of August. The Karma dance symbolizes the bringing of green branches of the forest in the spring. Sometimes a tree is actually set up in the village and people dance round it. The dance is filled with breath of trees.

The men leap forward to a rapid roll of drums. Bending low to the ground the women dance, their feet moving in perfect rhythm to and fro, until the group of singers advances towards them.

The Majhwars of Sarguja district dance the Karma towards the beginning and the end of the rainy season. The Gonds and the Baigas of Mandla and Bilaspur districts dance it at any time they wish. The Baigas, the Jhumies, the Kanwars and the Gonds of Baghelkhand area perform this dance to the accompaniment of the Thumki, the Payri, the Chhalla and the Jhumki instruments. The Sirki, the Ghatwar, the Jhumar, the Ektaria, the Pendehar, the Dohoari, the Tegwani and the Lahaki are some of the sub-varieties of the Karma dance.

There are other variants of the Karma. The songs associated with these variants differ with each pattern. The Thadi, the Lahaki, the Khalha, the Jhumar and the Jharpat are the variations of Baiga Adivasis dance. The Karma seems to have been the oldest dance form of the Adivasis of Madhya Pradesh. It is the only dance which is common to the many ethnic groups of India.

Kaksar Dance: The dance of the Hill Marias of the Abujhmar mountains is quite different. In one of their dance-forms they carry dummy horses on their shoulders and move slowly into a wide circle.

Kaksar is a festival dance, performed by the Abhujmaria of Bastar. Prior to the rains, the Maria cultivators in every village worship the deity for reaping a rich harvest. To invoke the blessing of the deity, Kaksar, a group dance, in which young boys and girls take part, is performed. Boys put on a peculiar costume of a long white robe while girls are clad in all their finery. The dance presents to both girls and boys, a unique opportunity to choose their life partners, and marriage is enthusiastically celebrated afterwards. There is a rhythm and melody in this dance. The melodious music, the tinkling of the bells combine to create an atmosphere of spell and enchantment.

Chaitra Festival Dance: The Chaitra festival dance is another famous dance of the Gonds of Bastar district; it is performed after the harvest to thank goddess Annapurna for the harvest already gathered and to seek her blessings for the next crop. Men and women dance in a circle, in semi-circles or in rows; all dancers hold each other's waist.

A peacock feather on the head is a distinctive mark and the dancers wear colourful costumes, adorning themselves with garlands of shells and pearls. As the dancers go round in rhythmic movements, their feet beat to the music of the Shehnai, Nagada, Timki, Tapri, Dholak and Maduri. Sometimes, the Singha and Kohuk; wind instruments are also played.

The Rina is the women's dance. It is called Tapadi among the Baigas. The Gond women of Mandla district start the Rina just after the festival of Diwali.

Sua or Sugga Dance: The Sua or Sugga dance of the women of Chhattisgarh and the Mikal Hills is significant for its elegance and grace. The word 'Sua' means a parrot. The women take recourse to this dance a month in advance of the festival of Diwali. While dancing, the women lift their feet in imagination of a parrot-walk, then bend and jerk their heads in bird-like fashion to the clapping of hands. Groups of girls often go on long trips to the adjoining villages to display their excellence in this dance.

Similarly they receive groups of girls visiting their own village. They prepare a wooden Sugga (a parrot) and place it on an earthen pot covered with paddy shoots. One of the girls carries the pot on her head and stands as a revolving figure in the middle of the group to face the dancing row when the opposite row of the girls alternatively stops. In this dance no instrument is used with the exception of a wooden clapper named Thiski is played to provide rhythm, where the Gonds and the Baigas predominate.

The folk-dances of the hilly tracts of the Vindhyas are more indigenous and recreational. Not a single ceremonial occasion passes in any community without dance and music. The Bhils who inhabit the Vindhya ranges and the banks of the Narmada are traditionally prone to their Bhagoriah and Gavar dances. Their instruments are an ordinary Mandal (big drum) and a Thali (brass plate). Hundreds of men and women join and move in a circle with wild shouts and lusty songs to the noisy abandon of the beat of drums. The Bhagoriah is typical of ecstasy and vibrating spectacle. Men waving bows and arrows synchronize their movements and stamping of feet with verve. During the Holi festival in Phalguna (Feburary) the Bhils and the Garasias perform a dance called the Ger. The women of both these tribes also dance the Loor. They form a circle and then holding their hands, they dance the Loor with forward and backward movements. In the Pali dance, the women form two rows. The Duipali, the Pachmundya Pali and the Ondi-Chiti Pali are the other forms of the Pali dance.

Folk-dances of Nomadic Tribes: Some of the indigenous folk-dances of Madhya Pradesh are by nomadic tribes like the Banjara and the Kanjar of Bhopal commissionary. In this area, one comes across a dance form known as Lehangi. In the middle of the rainy season when nature comes to bloom the Lehangi is danced by young men over the beat of sticks which they hold in their hands. The Kanjars are professional acrobats. They dance with full poise and acrobatic tricks.

On the Rakhi festival, the Banjaras of Nimad dance the Lehangi. When the festival of Dussehra approaches they start dancing Garbi and Dandia. Banjara dancers have a remarkable similarity in their mode. The men accompany the women either with songs or instruments. The Banjara women are heavily decked with silver jewellery and wrapped in colourful clothes of contrasting embroidery and tiny inset of scintillating mirrors. In the Lota dance, with all the ornaments and heavy clothes, they balance big-size metal pots on their heads as they swing in a liner or a circular formation.

Matki Dance: The tableland of Malwa has comparatively very few dances. On wedding occasions, the countryside women of this part perform the 'Matki' dance with an earthen pot balanced on the head, the Matki is mostly danced solo. Sometimes just for merriment a couple of women join the main dancer who usually dances with a veil on her face. The two other variations of the Matki are the Aada and Khada Nach.

Phulpati Dance: The Phulpati is another dance, exclusively for unmarried girls. It is a dance of the semi-rural womenfolk. The agriculturist class of Malwa is not very much inclined to any dance by nature. During the Holi festival the revelers cannot restrain themselves from coming out with some sort of dance movements to the uneven manipulation of drums.

Grida Dance: When rabi crops sway in the fields in full bloom, the parties from different villages join together and perform the Grida dance. It continues from morning till evening. The host village returns the visit next year by going to the village of their guests of the preceding year. The dance has three distinct phases: (1) Sela - The feet movements are slow and comparatively rigid. (2) Selalarki - The feet movements become brisker and faster. (3) Selabhadoni - With the acceleration of the tempo, every limb of the body begins to sway in mood of exaltation.

The Attire: The men wear white muslin turbans or occasionally silk ones. The turban is adorned with a coronet of peacock feather stems. Down to the waist they wear a close white Saluka or blouse, below a dhoti of small width coming down to the knees, the end of which hangs loosely behind. On their necks hang necklaces of silver or gold coins or corals. Their hands are adorned with silver bangles and their feet with heavy brass or iron, boat-shaped ornaments which tinkle to the timing of the rhythm. In their right hand they hold a staff, in their left a white kerchief or peacock feathers.

The costumes of the musicians are different from those of the dancers. They put on a shirt or a jacket and coloured turbans; they do not use cowries.

The women wear a coloured dhoti, wound close round the body down to the knees, one end of which goes up across their breasts to their backs. The knot of their hair is adorned with a coronet of palm or other leaves behind which hangs a net of corals. From their necks also hangs a chain of coins or corals. Besides the necklaces of coins or corals they wear silver hansali also. In their ears, they wear heavy silver ear-rings from which hang small slender silver chains. Besides, they wear bahunta (armlets) on their arms, silver bangles on their wrists and perry or todar round their ankles. While dancing, in their right hand they hold thiski (a clapper) and in their left a coloured kerchief.

3

Government and Politics

INTRODUCTION

Madhya Pradesh has a 230-seat state legislative assembly. The state also sends 40 members to the Parliament of India: 29 are elected to the Lok Sabha (Lower House) and 11 to the Rajya Sabha (Upper House).

The constitutional head of the state is the Governor, appointed by the President of India. The executionary powers lie with the Chief Minister, who is the elected leader of the state legislature. As of 2016, the current governor is Anandiben Patel, and the chief minister is Shivraj Singh Chouhan of the Bharatiya Janata Party (BJP).

The dominant political parties in the state are the Bharatiya Janata Party (BJP) and the Indian National Congress. Unlike in many of the neighbouring states, the small or regional parties have not had much success in the state elections.

In the November 2013 state elections, the BJP won an absolute majority of 165 seats, defeating Congress which won 58 seats. Bahujan Samaj Party is the third major party in the state legislature, with 4 seats while others won 3 seats.

Administration

Madhya Pradesh state is made up of 52 Districts, which are grouped into 10 divisions. As of 2013, the state has 52 jila (district) panchayats, 369 tehsil, 313 janpad panchayats/blocks, and 23043 gram (village) panchayats. The municipalities in the state include 16 Nagar Nigams, 100 Nagar Palikas and 264 Nagar Panchayats.

DISTRICT FUNCTIONARY

The Corporation is providing support to the farmers of entire Madhya Pradesh through its all offices located in all forty-five-district headquarters. To streamline the facility being provided to the farmers and to give more transparency on the functionality of the Corporation the Corporation has computerized its all forty-five district-offices and linked with headquarters for quick and smooth flow of orders as well as information.

Directorate of Agricultural Engineering: Mechanization of agriculture is an essential input to the modern agriculture. It enhances productivity, besides reducing human drudgery and cost of cultivation. Mechanization also helps in improving utilization efficiencies of other inputs. As compared to some of the neighbouring states, pace of mechanization of agriculture in Madhya Pradesh is not to the desired level. To achieve this objective, **Directorate of Agricultural Engineering** was established during the year 1989, with a modest staff of 1709, which has been reduced to 1270 after formation of Chhattisgarh State.

The main thrust of Directorate, has been to help the farmers to raise the farm productivity through custom hiring of machines and introduction of improved farm machinery and equipments.

Objectives:

(A) Offer Custom Hiring Services.

(B) Popularization of Improved Agricultural Implements and Machinery, Through Demonstrations in Farmers' Fields.

(C) Subsidy Programme of Tractors, Power Tillers and Improved Agricultural Implements.

(D) Quality Check of Sprinkler and Drip Irrigation System being distributed to the Farmers.

(E) Developing of Prototype of New Agricultural Implements and their Manufacture in Departmental Workshops.

(F) Training to Village Artisans on Manufacturing of Agricultural Implements.

Offer Custom Hiring Services

Machines are hired to the farmers, and other institutions for following activities;

(1) *Deep Ploughing:* Deep ploughing and turning the soils during summers helps in restoring the fertility of soils besides eradicating the harmful weeds, bacterias and nematodes etc. present in the soil. Such ploughing is done by tractors with Mould Board ploughs. The Directorate owns a fleet of 37 chain type tractors with heavy duty Mold Board ploughs.

It is worth mentioning that these machines are available only with this Directotare. These machines carry out deep ploughing during hot dry summer conditions upto a depth of 12" to 14". Machines are hired to the farmers at the rates approved by State Government. Now bank loan is also available for this activity

(2) *Land Leveling:* Directorate owns a fleet of 76 bulldozers, which are hired to the farmers on custom basis at the rates approved by the State Government for levelling, bunding terracing of agricultural lands. These machines are also hired for construction of water harvesting structures. Machines are also hired to government and semi-government agencies, private firms etc. for non-agricultural purposes at rates, which are higher than rates prescribed for agricultural purposes. Facility of bank loan is available for this activity.

(3) *Light Cultivation and other Farm Operations:* Directorate owns a fleet of 135 wheel tractors with following equipments for light cultivation and other agricultural operations;

* M.B.Ploughs
* Disc Ploughs
* Cultivators
* Seed -Cum-Ferti.Drill
* Zero Till Seed-Cum-Ferti.Drill
* Paddy Transplanter
* Inclined Plate Planters
* Garlic Planters
* Potato Planters
* Sugarcane Cutter Planters
* Raised Bed Planters
* Reapers
* Threshers
* Power Tillers etc.

These machine are hired to the farmers on custom basis at the rates prescribed by the Government for completion of different farm operations in a short duration. Rotavator is an equipment, which helps in preparation of seedbed after Kharif crops, like soybean and paddy etc. in one go.

Thus it helps in conserving the residual moisture available in soil and reduces the cost of cultivation. Due to the efforts of this Directorate this equipment has become immensely popular in the State and now nearly 500 farmers own this machine.

(4) *Yield Testing and Flushing of Bores:* Directorate owns a fleet of 33 Air-compressors, with maching accessories. These machines are hired to the farmers for yield testing of tubewells and cleaning/flushing of existing tubewells. These machines are also used for deepening of wells through blasting.

Popularization of Improved Agricultural Implements through Demonstrations

Under Central Sector Scheme of 'Demonstration of Newly Developed Agricultural Equipment Including Horticultural Equipments at farmers fields', newly developed agricultural/ horticultural equipments and machinery are procured and their demonstrations are carried out at farmerts' fields.

The effect of these demonstrations has been very positive, with the result farmers have now started opting for improved farm machines like; rotavators, seed-cum-ferti drills, paddy transplaners, garlic planters, weeders, straw reapers, threshers and mini-rice mill etc.

Subsidy Programme

1. *Subsidy on Small Tractors:* Under Centrally Sponsored Macro-Management Scheme in which sharing pattern between Union Government and State Government is in the ratio of 90:10, all category of farmers are eligible foe subsidy on purchase of small tractors upto 35 P.T.O. Horsepower upto Rs.30, 000/- subject to maximum of 25% of the cost Since availability of tractors in Madhya Pradesh is comparatively low, farmers are coming forward in large number to avail the benefit of this programme. The programme is tied with institutional credit.
2. *Subsidy on Power Tillers:* Power tiller is a small tractor which can be used as a prime mower for operating different farm machines like rotavator, seed drill etc. in small fields, gardens and orchards. This is a very useful equipment for small farmers who cannot afford a tractor. On purchase of power tiller, subsidy upto Rs.30, 000/- subject to maximum of 25% of the cost is admissible to all category of farmers. The scheme is gradually picking up in rice growing areas and in areas where farmers have orchards.
3. *Subsidy on Improved Agricultural Implements:* Under Centrally Sponsored Macro-Management Scheme, subsidy

upto 25 % of the cost on improved bullock drawn and power operated implements and farm machines is admissible to all category of farmers. Under this programme, nearly 1.50 lakh bullock drawn and hand operated improved agricultural equipments are being distributed to the farmers of the State annualy, with the result we have been able to reduce human drudgery and enhancing production and productivity besides reducing the cost of cultivation. The State is proud to be at the top in distribution of improved agricultural equipments in the country. Some of the improved agricultural implements, which are included in the subsidy programme, are;

Bullock Drawn

1. Mould Board Plough, 2. Improved Bakhar, 3. Seed-cum-ferti drills, 4. Weeder, 5. Groundnut Digger 6. Potato planter, 7. Garlic planter, 8. Bund former, 9. Groundnut decorticator, 10. Maize sheller, 11.Low lift water Device etc.

Power Drawn/Power Operated

1. Ploughs, 2.Harrows, 3.Rotavators, 4.Seed-Cum-ferti.drills, 5.Inclined plate planters, 6.Self propelled paddy tranplanters, 7.Multicrop threshers, 8.Reapers, 9.Mini dal mill, 10.Mini rice mill etc.

GOVERNMENT AND POLITICS

For decades, Madhya Pradesh has been a prosperous state. It has more or less a stable governance.Madhya Pradesh government and politics has initiated e-governance in its various sectors of governance with the advancement of computer and information technology.

Basic Structure of Madhya Pradesh Government and Politics: There is only one house in Madhya Pradesh Government - the Madhya Pradesh Legislative Assembly (Vidhan Sabha).

It consists of 60 members. Therefore, the basic structure of administration in Madhya Pradesh government and politics is the same as in other Indian states. The Lok Sabha consists of 2 seats - the lower house of Parliament and the Rajya Sabha consists of 1 seat - the upper house of Parliament.

Important positions in Madhya Pradesh government and politics:

- Chief Minister: The head of government is the Chief Minister. He has most of the executive powers in his hands.
- Governor: The head of the state is the Governor. He is appointed by the President of India. His or her post is ceremonial in nature with not much of executive powers.
- Ministers: A group of ministers help the Chief Minister to execute administrative tasks. Each of them has independent power.

Political Parties in Madhya Pradesh Government and Politics: The leading political parties in Madhya Pradesh Politics are Indian National Congress, Bharatiya Janata Party, Jiti Jitayi Politics, Madhya Pradesh Kisan Mazdoor Adivasi Kranti Dal, Madhya Pradesh Vikas Congress, and Pragatisheel Bahujan Samaj Party.

Current Scenario in Madhya Pradesh Government and Politics: The current Chief Minister of Madhya Pradesh is Shivraj Singh Chouhan. The current Governor of Madhya Pradesh is Dr. Balram Jakhar. The present Chief Secretary is RC Sahni.

The present government is led by Shivraj Singh Chouhan, a BJP party worker.

Prior to Shivraj Singh Chouhan, Babulal Gaur and Uma Bharti from the same BJP were the chief ministers of the state. The state was governed by Mr. Digvijay Singh of the Congress party before the last election.

The two major political parties in Madhya Pradesh are Indian National Congress and Bharatiya Janata Party (BJP).

Boards and Commissions

Madhya Pradesh Boards and Commissions include 10 Commissions and 55 Boards. Some of the important Madhya Pradesh Boards and Commissions are Madhya Pradesh Public Service Commission, Madhya Pradesh Human Rights Commission and Madhya Pradesh State Agricultural Marketing Board. Some quick facts about Madhya Pradesh Boards and Commissions are given below.

Madhya Pradesh Boards and Commissions:

- Madhya Pradesh Electricity Board
- Madhya Pradesh State Agricultural Marketing Board
- Madhya Pradesh Labor Welfare Board
- Secondary Education Board
- Madhya Pradesh State Planning Board
- Madhya Pradesh State Housing Board
- Madhya Pradesh Vocational Examination Board
- Madhya Pradesh Khadi and Village Industries Board
- Madhya Pradesh Electricity Regulatory Commission
- Madhya Pradesh State Scheduled Tribes Commission
- Madhya Pradesh State Scheduled Caste Commission
- Madhya Pradesh State Consumer Redressal Commission
- Madhya Pradesh State Women Commission
- Madhya Pradesh State Backward Classes Commission
- Madhya Pradesh State Minorities Commission

Some important phone numbers of Madhya Pradesh Boards and Commissions:

Madhya Pradesh Public Service Commission:

- Chairman: 2702219
- Secretary: 2702979

Madhya Pradesh State Election Commission:

- State Election Commissioner: 2551535
- Secretary: 2555527

Madhya Pradesh Human Rights Commission:

- Chairman: 2764505

Madhya Pradesh Electricity Regulatory Commission:

- Chairman: 2557819

Madhya Pradesh State Scheduled Tribes Commission

- Chairman: 2542700
- Member: 2660876

Madhya Pradesh State Scheduled Castes Commission

- Chairman: 2533343
- Secretary: 2533847

Madhya Pradesh State Consumer Redressal Commission:

- Chairman: 2554270
- Member: 2763024
- Registrar: 2553722

Madhya Pradesh State Women Commission:

- Chairman: 2531427
- Member Secretary: 2545678

Madhya Pradesh State Backward Classes Commission

- Chairman: 2660638
- Secretary: 2660637

Madhya Pradesh State Minorities Commission:

- Chairman: 2737361
- Secretary: 2737362, 2540989

Madhya Pradesh Electricity Board:

- Chairman: 2663251

Madhya Pradesh State Agricultural Marketing Board

- Chairman: 2551765, 2574384
- Managing Director: 2553429

Madhya Pradesh Labor Welfare Board

- Chairman: 2572753

Secondary Education Board:

- Chairman: 2551544
- Secretary: 2551650

Madhya Pradesh State Planning Board

- Chairman: 2551713

Madhya Pradesh State Housing Board

- Chairman: 2571772
- Commissioner: 2551804

Madhya Pradesh Vocational Examination Board

- Chairman: 2553499

ELECTIONS IN MADHYA PRADESH

Elections in Madhya Pradesh, a state in India are conducted in accordance with the Constitution of India. The Assembly of Madhya Pradesh creates laws regarding the conduct of local body elections unilaterally while any changes by the state legislature to the conduct of state level elections need to be approved by the Parliament of India. In addition, the state legislature may be dismissed by the Parliament according to Article 356 of the Indian Constitution and President's rule may be imposed.

Main Political Parties Over The Years

BJP: Bharatiya Janata Party, BJS or JS: Bharatiya Jana Sangh (precursor of BJP), BSP: Bahujan Samaj Party

INC: Congress or Congress(Indira), SWA: Swatantra Party, JNP or JP or JD: Janata Party/Dal,

BLD: Bharatiya Lok Dal (Janata Party's official handle in 1977), Ind: Independent

Lok Sabha Elections

- 1951: Congress: 28 out of 29. In 1951, Gwalior region was not in MP but part of Madhya Bharat. There was Rewa-Satna territory in Vindhya Pradesh, which later merged with MP. Vidarbha was part of MP until merging with Maharashtra in 1960.

- 1957: Total: 35. Cong: 34, Hindu Maha Sabha (HMS): 1. Though Nagpur was capital of MP in 1957, Lok Sabha seats in Vidarbha (including Nagpur) had moved to Bombay State as per the impending realignment of states on linguistic basis.
- 1962: Total: 36. Cong: 24, BJS: 3, PSP (Praja Socialist): 3
- 1967: Total: 37. Cong: 25, BJS: 10, SWA: 1, Ind: 1
- 1971: Total: 37. Cong: 21, BJS: 11, Ind: 4
- 1977: Total: 40. Janata Party: 38. Cong: 1 (Chhindwara), Independent: 1 (Guna)
- 1980: Congress (Indira): 35/40, Janata Party: 4
- 1984: Congress: 40/40. BJP: Zero.
- 1989: BJP: 27, Congress: 8, JD: 3
- 1991: Cong: 27, BJP: 12, BSP: 1
- 1996: BJP: 27, Cong: 8, BSP: 2
- 1998: Total: 40. BJP: 30, Congress: 10.
- 1999: Total: 40. BJP: 29, Congress: 11
- 2004: Total: 29 (Chhattisgarh state was carved out of MP, and it got 11 seats out of Old MP's 40 seats.) BJP: 25. INC: 4
- 2009: Total-29. BJP: 16, Cong: 12, BSP: 1.
- 2014: Total: 29. BJP: 27, Congress: 2 (Chhindwara and Guna)

Vidhan Sabha Elections

- 1967: Total: 296. Cong: 167, BJS: 78, Swatantra: 7, SSP (Socialists): 10.
- 1972: Total: 296. Cong: 220, BJS: 48
- 1977: Total: 320. Janata Party: Around 220-240. Congress: 60-70. (Chief Ministers: Kailash Joshi, Virender Saklecha, Sunder Lal Patwa)
- 1980: Total: 320. Cong: 246, BJP: 60 (CM: Arjun Singh)
- 1985: Total: 320. Congress: 250, (CMs: Arjun Singh, Motilal Vora) BJP: 58. # Ref for 1985 -

- 1990: Total: 320. BJP: 220, Congress: 56, Janata Dal: 28. (CM: Sunder Lal Patwa. March 1990 - December 1992)
- 1993: Total: 320. Congress: 174, BJP: 117 (CM: Digvijay Singh of Congress)
- 1998: Total: 320. Congress: 161, BJP: 123 (CM: Digvijay Singh)
- Chhattisgarh state was carved out of MP, so the 2003 assembly no longer had 320 seats.
- 2003: Total: 230. BJP: 172, Congress: 39 (CMs: Uma Bharti, Babulal Gaur, Shivraj Singh Chouhan)
- 2008: Total: 230. BJP: 143. (CM: Shivraj Singh Chouhan)
- 2013: Total:230; BJP:165, Congress: 58, BSP: 4 (Chief Minister(s): Shivraj Singh Chouhan)

GOVERNMENT OF MADHYA PRADESH

The Government of Madhya Pradesh also known as the State Government of Madhya Pradesh, or locally as State Government, is the supreme governing authority of the Indian state of Madhya Pradesh and its 51 districts. It consists of an executive, led by the Governor of Madhya Pradesh, a judiciary and a legislative branch.

Like other states in India, the head of state of Madhya Pradesh is the Governor, appointed by the President of India on the advice of the Central government. His or her post is largely ceremonial. The Chief Minister is the head of government and is vested with most of the executive powers. Bhopal is the capital of Madhya Pradesh, and houses the Madhya Pradesh Vidhan Sabha (Legislative Assembly) and the secretariat. The Madhya Pradesh High Court, located in Jabalpur, has jurisdiction over the whole state.

The present legislature of Madhya Pradesh is unicameral. The legislative house, Madhya Pradesh Vidhan Sabha consists 230 Members of Legislative Assembly (MLA) elected directly from single-seat constituencies and one nominated member. Its term is 5 years, unless sooner dissolved.

On 1 Feb, 2016 the Madhya Pradesh banned the use of English, effectively Hindi will be used for all official purposes, and issued instructions to officials not to harass employees who do not know English. On 4 December 2017, Madhya Pradesh Assembly unanimously passed a Bill awarding death to those found guilty of raping girls aged 12 and below

MADHYA PRADESH LEGISLATIVE ASSEMBLY

The Madhya Pradesh Vidhan Sabha or the Madhya Pradesh Legislative Assembly is the unicameral state legislature of Madhya Pradesh state in central-India. The seat of the Vidhan Sabha is at Bhopal, the capital of the state. It is housed in the *Vidhan Bhavan*, an imposing building located at the centre of the Capital Complex in the Arera Hill locality of Bhopal city. The term of the Vidhan Sabha is five years, unless dissolved sooner. Presently, it comprises 230 members who are directly elected from single-seat constituencies and one nominated member. The present Speaker is Sitasharan Sharma (BJP) who was elected on 9 January 2014. Rajendra Kumar Singh (INC) was elected Deputy Speaker on 10 January 2014.

History

The history of the Madhya Pradesh legislature can be traced back to 1913, as the Central Provinces Legislative Council was formed on 8 November of this year. Later, the Government of India Act, 1935 provided for the elected Central Provinces Legislative assembly. The first elections to the Central Provinces Legislative Assembly were held in 1937.

After Indian independence in 1947, the erstwhile province of Central Provinces and Berar, along with a number of princely statesmerged with the Indian Union, became a new state, Madhya Pradesh. The strength of the legislative assembly of this state was 184.

The present-day Madhya Pradesh state came into existence on 1 November 1956 following the reorganisation of states. It was created by merging the erstwhile Madhya Pradesh (without the Marathi speaking areas, which were merged with Bombay state), Madhya Bharat, Vindhya Pradesh and Bhopal states. The strengths of the legislative assemblies of Madhya Bharat, Vindhya Pradesh and Bhopal were 79, 48 and 23 respectively. On 1 November 1956 the legislative assemblies of all four erstwhile states were also merged to form the reorganised Madhya Pradesh Vidhan Sabha. The tenure of this first Vidhan Sabha was very short, and it was dissolved on 5 March 1957.

The first elections to the Madhya Pradesh Vidhan Sabha were held in 1957 and the second Vidhan Sabha was constituted on 1 April 1957. Initially, the strength of the Vidhan Sabha was 288, which was later enhanced to 321, including one nominated member. On 1 November 2000, a new state, Chhattisgarh, was carved out of Madhya Pradesh state. As a result, the strength of the Vidhan Sabha was reduced to 231, including a nominated member. The present house, the fourteenth Vidhan Sabha, was constituted on 11 December 2013.

The present building was designed by Charles Correa in 1967, and it was the recipient of the Aga Khan Award for Architecture in 1998.

4

Language and Literature

LANGUAGES

The official language of the state is Hindi. In addition Marathi is spoken by a substantial number of the population since the state was home to several important and prestigious Maratha states. The state in fact has the highest concentration of Marathi people outside Maharashtra. Several regional variants are spoken, which are considered by some to be dialects of Hindi, and by others to be distinct but related languages. Among these dialects are Malvi in Malwa, Nimadi in Nimar, Bundeli in Bundelkhand, and Bagheli in Bagelkhand and the southeast, and Rajasthani in the area near to Rajasthan. Each of these languages has dialects of its own. Other languages include Telugu, Bhilodi (Bhili), Gondi, Korku, Kalto (Nahali), and Nihali (Nahali), all spoken by tribal groups.

The following languages are taught in schools in Madhya Pradesh under the Three Language Formula:

First Language: Hindi, Urdu, English, Oriya, Marathi, Sindhi, Tamil, Telugu, Punjabi, Bengali, Gujarati, Malayalam, Kannada

Second Language: Hindi, Urdu, English

Third Language: Hindi, English, Sanskrit, Marathi, Urdu, Punjabi, Sindhi, Bengali, Gujarati, Telugu, Tamil, Arabic, Malayalam, Persian, French, Russian, Oriya, Kannada

THE PEOPLE

Madhya Pradesh has the largest population of Scheduled Tribes of all states and a high proportion of Scheduled Castes. Of the total 45 districts, 23 are predominantly tribal. The major tribes of Madhya Pradesh are Gonds, Bhils, Oraons, Korkens, and Kols. The state presents in all a varied matrix of tribal culture ranging from animists and fowlers to advanced cultivators and factory workers.

Away from the tribal stock of Madhya Pradesh the rest of the population consists of Hindu communities. They include Rajput landholders, traditional merchant classes and established agriculturists such as the Ahirs, the Khatis, the Kunbis, the Lodhis, the Malis and others. The industries and factories in the urban areas have drawn labour from all the classes. A small percentage of Parsis, Muslims and Jains also add to the racial mosaic of Madhya Pradesh.

By its geographical position, Madhya Pradesh has remained exposed to cultural influences. The central region of the state was directly under the Indo-Aryan culture. The Vindhyas sheltered primitive tribes since the early dawn of history. No communication was possible with the south from the north because their existence was an effective barrier until the Marathas entered Malwa and its nearby territories. On account of the sturdy barrier of these mountainous ranges, all the racial movements, incursion and migration, took place in central Madhya Pradesh, from the Gangetic plain, Rajasthan and Gujarat through the gap in one of its arms. Fertile lands of the state have drawn people from distant directions.

The interpenetration of the culture of the hills and the forests and the plains has been going on from time immemorial. It is only in the lower part of Madhya Pradesh that the Adivasis maintain their indigenous culture. The socio economic condition of the people has improved considerably since independence. People have become conscious of their rights. The economy of the state has developed to a desired satisfaction. Social changes were bound to occur in the tribal section of the population of the state. Social welfare agencies made them aware of many things. There are instances of adapting traditional Hindu manners and ritualistic patterns by some of the Adivasis

PREDOMINANT LANGUAGES

The predominant language of the region is Hindi. In addition to standard Hindi, several regional variants are spoken, which are considered by some to be dialects of Hindi, and by others to be distinct but related languages. Among these languages are Malvi in Malwa, Nimadi in Nimar, Bundeli in Bundelkhand, and Bagheli and Avadhi in Bagelkhand and the southeast. Each of these languages or dialects has dialects of its own. Other languages include Bhilodi (Bhili), Gondi, and the isolate Kalto (Nahali), all spoken by tribal groups. Due to rule of Marathas, Marathi is spoken by a substantial number of people.

TRIBES

The major tribes of Madhya Pradesh are Gonds, Bhils, Oraons, Korkens, and Kols. The tribal culture of Madhya Pradesh is mixed with traces of the Dravidians, the Mundas and the Scythians. There are forest-dwellers such as the Abujhmarias, the hunters and the gawkier such as the Korwas and the Pandhis. There are the Khaiwars and the Panikas who depend on indigenous methods of cultivation. There are even many others whose profession is singing and dancing such as the Mangetri Pradhans or the Nagachis or Bediyas. The state presents in all a varied matrix of tribal culture ranging from animists and fowlers to advanced cultivators and factory workers.

The Chhatlisgarh region of the state comprises Raigarh, Surgaja, Bilaspur, Durg and Raipur districts. It is found that the inhabitants of this area bestowed with many peculiarities. The 'Pradhans', the hereditary chroniclers are a bardic tribe of Chhatlisgarh and worship various Gods and Goddesses. The Gond rulers patronized them in the fourteenth century. The dialect spoken in the region is Chhatlisgarh. The soil is red and yellow and almost half of the area comes under rice cultivation.

The Indravati flows through the Bastar region and quite a large portion of this vast district is covered with jungle. The Murias of North Bastar are associated with institution of Ghotul which is a sort of dormitory for the young boys and girls of this tribe. The bison-horn Marias or the sing-Marias are settled to the south of the Indravati. They have very little communication with the Murias of the north. The Raja Murias or the Jagdalpur Murias consider themselves superior to other tribes. The Halbas are the near Hindu caste predominant all over the tract. Halbi which is their dialect had great impact over other dialects spoken in the region.

The wild and more primitive interior of Bastar is the rugged and mountainous terrain of **Abujhmar** in the west of Narayanpur Tehsil. The inhabitants here may eat any thing they like. Red ants is their favourite dish. Rats are eaten with pleasure and to full satisfaction.

The Abujhmarias have a strange wild appeal in their look as compared to the Murias of the plains. Women are generally seen bare-bosomed and men roam around wearing just a loin cloth. Only during festivals they add some more items to their dress. Boys don all kinds of finery. They wear red or white 'pagas' (turbans) with feathers tucked in their folds. The Hill Marias believe in slash and burn type of cultivation. Many places of Abujhmar are noted as un-surveyed. These areas are topographically rough and dense with a variety of living things.

The Dhurwas (Parjas) are the third largest Adivasi group in Baster following the Marias and the Murias. The tribe is concentrated in Dantewara and Konta. They border on most tehsils of Madhya Pradesh in the South.

The Bhils inhabit the districts of Dhar, Ratlam and Jhabua. A number of beliefs and superstitions admit them 'outside the Hindu social system'. The Bhil group constitutes the Bhilala, the Mankar, the Patlia, the Barela, the Nihal or Naik and the Rathia.

The Gond and Kol groups are found in Chhindwara. They are also settled by the rivers of Betul, among the hills of Seoni and Balaghat. They have an extensive legendary history of their past heroes. Tribals of Bastar come under this group. The Gonds are a great people with stirring memories and passionate poetry. They seem to have entered the wilds of Baster along the banks of the Godavari. In the fourteenth century they were the ruling class in many parts of central India. They built palaces, forts, tanks and lakes but owing to their over-simplicity and tolerance they failed to retain their establishments. Towards the end of the eighteenth century they were found scattered into many tribes.

The Baigas are a class of priests among the Gonds. They are the people who know all about evil spirits and can avoid them by performing magical rites. In Mandla district there is a small tract called Baiga Chak, known for its Baiga settlement. The Baigas have now changed considerably.

The Pradhans are the musicians of the Gond and the Baigas. If a Baiga is not available to a Gond, a Pradhan is called for performing the rites. The Korkus are confined to a small portion in the Narmada valley. Some of them have taken to work in the coal-mines around Chhindwara.

The Savaras are mostly inhabited in Sheopur (Morena district), Isagarh, Narval (Gwalior district) and Bhilsa. This group also combines Saharia and Sour. Among other tribes are the Kols of Maikal hills who are mainly agriculturists and wage-earners in factories, the Korwas and the Oraons of Raigarh and Surguja districts, the Bharias of Patalkot and the adjoining areas in Chhindwara and the Binjhwars of Bilaspur.

The Banjaras are nomadic people settled in some parts of the Narmada valley. They have a rich folklore of their own and a strong community sense.

5

Geography and Flora & Fauna

GEOGRAPHY

Madhya Pradesh in Hindi can be translated to Central Province, and it is located in the geographic heart of India. The state straddles the Narmada River, which runs east and west between the Vindhya and Satpura ranges; these ranges and the Narmada are the traditional boundary between the north and south of India. The state is bordered on the west by Gujarat, on the northwest by Rajasthan, on the northeast by Uttar Pradesh, on the east by Chhattisgarh, and on the south by Maharashtra.

Madhya Pradesh comprises several linguistically and culturally distinct regions, including:

- *Malwa:* A plateau region in the northwest of the state, north of the Vindhya Range, with its distinct language and culture. Indore is the major city of the region, while Bhopal lies on the edge of Bundelkhand region. Ujjain is a town of historical importance.
- *Nimar (Nemar):* The western portion of the Narmada River valley, lying south of the Vindhyas in the southwest portion of the state.

- *Bundelkhand:* A region of rolling hills and fertile valleys in the northern part of the state, which slopes down toward the Indo-Gangetic plain to the north. Gwalior is an historic centre of the region.
- *Chambal:* The north-western region. A mountainous region rich in red, soft, and fragile sandstone. The climate is harsh, and the area is known for murderous pirates who were active in hundreds in the late 1900s.
- *Baghelkhand:* A hilly region in the northeast of the state, which includes the eastern end of the Vindhya Range.
- *Mahakoshal (Mahakaushal):* The southeastern portion of the state, which includes the eastern end of the Narmada river valley and the eastern Satpuras. Jabalpur is the most important city in the region.
- *Central Vindhya and Satpura Region:* Which has most of the central Narmada river valley and watershed, and has the highest point in the state—Dhupgarh in Pachmarhi.

The Malwa region occupies a plateau in western Madhya Pradesh and south-eastern Rajasthan (between 21°102 N 73°452 E and 25°102 N 79°142 E), with Gujarat in the west. To the south and east is the Vindhya Range and to the north is the Bundelkhand upland.

The plateau is an extension of the Deccan Traps, formed between 60 and 68 million years ago at the end of the Cretaceous period. In this region the main classes of soil are black, brown and *bhatori* (stony) soil. The volcanic, clay-like soil of the region owes its black colour to the high iron content of the basalt from which it formed. The soil requires less irrigation because of its high capacity for moisture retention. The other two soil types are lighter and have a higher proportion of sand.

The average elevation of the plateau is 500 m. Some of the peaks over 800 m high are at Sigar (881 m), Janapav (854 m) and Ghajari (810 m). The plateau generally slopes towards the north. The western part of the region is drained by the Mahi River, while the Chambal River drains the central part, and the Betwa River and the headwaters of the Dhasan and Ken rivers drain the east.

The Shipra River is of historical importance because of the Simhasth mela, held every 12 years. Other notable rivers are Parbati, Gambhir and Choti Kali Sindh. Malwa's elevation gives it a mild, pleasant climate; a cool morning wind, the *karaman*, and an evening breeze, the *Shab-e-Malwa*, make the summers less harsh.

The Vindhya Range marks the southern boundary of the plateau, and is the source of many rivers of the region.

The year is popularly divided into three seasons: summer, the rains, and winter. Summers extends over the months of Chaitra to Jyestha (mid-March to mid-May). The average daily temperature during the summer months is 35 °C, which typically rises to around 40 °C on a few days.

The rainy season starts with the first showers of Aashaadha (mid-June) and extends to the middle of Ashvin (September). Most of the rain falls during the southwest monsoon spell, and ranges from about 100 cm in the west to about 165 cm in the east. Indore and the immediately surrounding areas receive an average of 140 cm of rainfall a year.

The growing period lasts from 90 to 150 days, during which the average daily temperature is below 30 °C, but seldom falls below 20 °C. Winter is the longest of the three seasons, extending for about five months (mid-Ashvin to Phalgun, *i.e.*, October to mid-March). The average daily temperature ranges from 15 °C to 20 °C, though on some nights it can fall as low as 7 °C. Some cultivators believe that an occasional winter shower during the months of Pausha and Maagha—known as Mawta—is helpful to the early summer wheat and germ crops.

The Sambhar is one of the most common wild animals found in the region. The region is part of the Kathiawar-Gir dry deciduous forests ecoregion.

Vegetation: The natural vegetation is tropical dry forest, with scattered teak *(Tectona grandis)* forests. The main trees are *Butea*, *Bombax*, *Anogeissus*, *Acacia*, *Buchanania* and

Boswellia. The shrubs or small trees include species of *Grewia, Ziziphus mauritiana, Casearia, Prosopis, Capparis, Woodfordia,* Phyllanthus, *and* Carissa.

Wildlife: Sambhar *(Cervus unicolor)*, Blackbuck *(Antilope cervicapra)*, and Chinkara *(Gazella bennettii)* are some common ungulates. During the last century, deforestation has happened at a fast rate, leading to environmental problems such as acute water scarcity and the danger that the region is being desertified.

Location in India

Madhya Pradesh literally means "Central Province", and is located in the geographic heart of India, between latitude 21.2°N-26.87°N and longitude 74°59'-82°06' E. The state straddles the Narmada River, which runs east and west between the Vindhya and Satpura ranges; these ranges and the Narmada are the traditional boundary between the north and south of India. The highest point in Madhya Pradesh is Dhupgarh, with an elevation of 1,350 m (4,429 ft).

The state is bordered on the west by Gujarat, on the northwest by Rajasthan, on the northeast by Uttar Pradesh, on the east by Chhattisgarh, and on the south by Maharashtra.

Climate

Madhya Pradesh has a subtropical climate. Like most of north India, it has a hot dry summer (April–June), followed by monsoon rains (July–September) and a cool and relatively dry winter. The average rainfall is about 1,371 mm (54.0 in). The southeastern districts have the heaviest rainfall, some places receiving as much as 2,150 mm (84.6 in), while the western and northwestern districts receive 1,000 mm (39.4 in) or less.

Ecology

According to the 2011 figures, the recorded forest area of the state is 94,689 km (36,560 sq mi) constituting 30.72% of the geographical area of the state. It constitutes 12.30% of the forest area of India. Legally this area has been classified into

"Reserved Forest" (65.3%), "Protected Forest" (32.84%) and "Unclassified Forest" (0.18%). Per capita forest area is 2,400 m^2 (0.59 acres) as against the national average of 700 m^2 (0.17 acres). The forest cover is less dense in the northern and western parts of the state, which contain the major urban centres. Variability in climatic and edaphic conditions brings about significant difference in the forest types of the state.

The major types of soils found in the state are:

- Black soil, most predominantly in the Malwa region, Mahakoshal and in southern Bundelkhand
- Red and yellow soil, in the Baghelkhand region
- Alluvial soil, in Northern Madhya Pradesh
- Laterite soil, in highland areas
- Mixed soil, in parts of the Gwalior and Chambal divisions.

DIVISIONS

Districts: Madhya Pradesh state is made up of 48 districts, which are grouped into nine divisions: Bhopal, Chambal, Gwalior, Indore, Jabalpur, Rewa, Sagar, and Ujjain Hosangabad (Smallest division of MP)

Districts: Anuppur, Ashoknagar, Balaghat, Barwani, Betul, Bhind, Bhopal, Burhanpur, Chhatarpur, Chhindwara, Damoh, Datia, Dewas, Dhar, Dindori, Guna, Gwalior, Harda, Hoshangabad, Indore, Jabalpur, Jhabua, Katni, Khandwa, Khargone, Mandla, Mandsaur, Morena, Narsinghpur, Neemuch, Panna, Raisen, Rajgarh, Ratlam, Rewa, Sagar, Satna, Sehore, Seoni, Shahdol, Shajapur, Sheopur, Shivpuri, Sidhi, Tikamgarh, Ujjain, Umaria, Vidisha.

MALWA

Largest city	Indore
22.42° N 75.54° E	
Main languages	Malvi, Hindi
Area	81,767 km^2
Population (2001)	18,889,000

Density	231/km^2
Birth rate (2001)	31.6
Death rate (2001)	10.3
Infant mortality rate (2001)	93.8

Malwa (Malvi) is a region in western India occupying a plateau of volcanic origin in the western part of Madhya Pradesh state. This region had been a separate political unit from the time of the Aryan tribe of *Malavas* until 1947, when the British Malwa Agency was merged into Madhya Bharat. Although political borders have fluctuated throughout history, the region has developed its own distinct culture and language. The plateau that forms a large part of the region is named the Malwa Plateau, after the region.

The average elevation of the Malwa plateau is 500 metres, and the landscape generally slopes towards the north. Most of the region is drained by the Chambal River and its tributaries; the western part is drained by the upper reaches of the Mahi River. Ujjain was the political, economic, and cultural capital of the region in ancient times, and Indore is presently the largest city and commercial centre. Overall, agriculture is the main occupation of the people of Malwa. The region has been one of the important producers of opium in the world. Cotton and soybeans are other important cash crops, and textiles are a major industry.

The region includes the Madhya Pradesh districts of Dewas, Dhar, Indore, Jhabua, Mandsaur, Neemuch, Rajgarh, Ratlam, Shajapur, Ujjain, and parts of Guna and Sehore, and the Rajasthan districts of Jhalawar and parts of Banswara and Chittorgarh. Politically and administratively, the definition of Malwa is sometimes extended to include the Nimar region south of the Vindhyas. Geologically, the Malwa Plateau generally refers to the volcanic upland south of the Vindhyas, which includes the Malwa region and extends east to include the upper basin of the Betwa and the headwaters of the Dhasan and Ken rivers. The region has a tropical climate with dry deciduous forests that are home to a number of tribes, most important of them being the Bhils. The culture of the region has had influences from Gujarati, Rajasthani and Marathi cultures. Malvi is the most commonly used language, especially in rural areas, while Hindi is widely understood in cities. Major places of tourist interest include Ujjain, Mandu, Maheshwar and Indore.

The first significant kingdom in the region was Avanti, an important power in western India by around 500 BC, when it was annexed by the Maurya Empire. The 5th-century Gupta period was a golden age in the history of Malwa. The dynasties of the Parmaras, the Malwa sultans, and the Marathas have ruled Malwa at various times. The region has given the world prominent leaders in the arts and sciences, including the poet and dramatist Kalidasa, the author Bhartrihari, the mathematicians and astronomers Varahamihira and Brahmagupta, and the polymath king Bhoj.

AGRO-CLIMATIC ZONES

Madhya Pradesh is divided into following agro-climatic zones:

- Kaimur Plateau and Satpura Hills
- Vindhyan Plateau (Hills)
- Narmada valley
- Wainganga valley
- Gird (Gwalior) Region
- Bundelkhand Region
- Satpura Plateau (Hills)
- Malwa Plateau
- Nimar Plateau
- Jhabua Hills

FLORA AND FAUNA

Madhya Pradesh is home to ten National Parks; Bandhavgarh National Park, Kanha National Park, Satpura National Park, Sanjay National Park, Madhav National Park, Van Vihar National Park, Mandla Plant Fossils National Park, Panna National Park, Pench National Park and Dinosaur

National Park, Dhar. There are also a number of nature reserves, including Amarkantak, Bagh Caves, Balaghat, Bori Natural Reserve, Ken Gharial, Ghatigaon, Kuno Palpur, Narwar, Chambal, Kukdeshwar, Narsinghgarh, Nora Dehi, Pachmarhi, Panpatha, Shikarganj, Patalkot, and Tamia. Pachmarhi Biosphere Reserve in Satpura Range, Amarkantak biosphere reserve and Panna National Park are three of the 18 biosphere reserves in India. Most of them are located in the Eastern Madhya Pradesh near Jabalpur.

Kanha, Bandhavgarh, Pench, Panna, and Satpura National Parks are managed as Project Tiger areas. The National Chambal Sanctuary is managed for conservation of gharial and mugger, river dolphin, smooth-coated otter and a number of turtle species. Ken-gharial and Son-gharial sanctuaries are managed for conservation of gharial and mugger. The barasingha is the state animal and the dudhraj is the state bird of Madhya Pradesh.

Based on composition, the teak and sal forests are the important forest formations in the state. Bamboo-bearing areas are widely distributed.

Flora and fauna of Madhya Pradesh

Foressystem in Madhya Pradesh

Madhya Pradesh is often called the *Heart of India*, is a state in central India. Its capital is Bhopal. Madhya Pradesh was originally the largest state in India until November 1, 2000 when the state of Chhattisgarh was carved out. It borders the states Uttar Pradesh, Chhattisgarh, Maharashtra, Gujarat and Rajasthan.

Forest statistics

Lying between latitude 21°04'N-26.87°N and longitude 74°02'-82°49' E, it is a reservoir of biodiversity. The geographical area of the state is 308,252 km^2 which constitutes 9.38% of the land area of the country. The forest area of the state is 95,221 km^{2}constituting 30.71% of the geographical area of the state and 12.44% of the forest area of the country. Legally this area has been classified into "Reserved Forest, Protected Forest and Unclassified Forest", which constitute 61.7%, 37.4% and 0.9% of the forest area respectively. Per capita forest area is 2,400 m^2 as against the national average of 700 m^2

As per the latest estimates of Forest Survey of India, published in the State of Forest Report (IFSR) 2011, the total forest cover of M.P. is 94,690 km^2., which is 30.71% of the land area - dense forest constituting 13.57% and open forest 11.22%.

One third of the state is forested and offers an exciting panorama of wildlife. In the national parks of Kanha, Bandhavgarh, Shivpuri and many others, one has the rare opportunity to see the tiger, bison and a wide variety of deer and antelope in sylvan surroundings. There are ten national parks and twenty five wildlife sanctuaries.

Forest composition

Central, eastern and southern parts of the state are rich, whereas northern and western parts are deficient in forest. Variability in climatic and edaphic conditions brings about significant difference in the forest types of the state. There are four important forest types: tropical moist, tropical dry, tropical thorn and subtropical broadleaved hill forests. The forest area can also be classified based on the composition of forest and terrain of the area. Based on composition, there are three important forest formations: teak forest, sal forest, and miscellaneous forest. Bamboo bearing areas are widely distributed in the state. To obviate pressure on the natural forests, plantations have been undertaken in forest and non forest areas to supplement the availability of fuel wood, small timber, fodder etc. Madhya Pradesh lost a good amount of forest recently when Chhattisgarh was carved out of it, as that region was the richest in forest.

Teak - *Tectona grandis* (common teak) is by far the most important timber species, with a wide distribution in Madhya Pradesh. It is found in following districts, namely Indore, Khandwa, Harda, Dewas, Sehore, Bhopal, Raisen, Vidisha, Betul, Hoshangaba, Chhindwara, Seoni, Balaghat, Mandla, Dindori, Shahdol, Umaria,Jabalpur, Damoh, Panna, Chhatarpur, Sagar, Satna, Rewa and Sidhi.

Sal - Sal or sakhu (*Shorea robusta*) is another important timber species in Madhya Pradesh. It is a large evergreen tree belonging to the family dipterocarpaceae. Sal forests of Madhya Pradesh are ecologically very important as they mark the termination of the great sal zone of the Central Indian Peninsula. Sal forests are located in the eastern part of the state while teak forests are localised in the western part. In between, there is a transition belt of mixed miscellaneous forests. There are also areas where teak and sal both species occur naturally mixed together forming unique ecosystem. Sal forests occupy an area of 7244 km^2, which is about 7.6% of the total forest area of the state. The sal forests are confined to the eastern part of the state in the districts Rewa, Sidhi, Umaria, Anuppur and southwards in districts Balaghat, Mandla, Dindori, and Jabalpur and occupy all ranges of Maikal and the highlands of Balaghat. Sal forests are also distributed in and around Pachmarhi in Hoshangabad and Chhindwara districts.

Mixed forests - The maximum forest cover in the state is that of mixed forests, which includes teak (*Tectona grandis*) or sal (*Shorea robusta*) mixed with other species like saja (*Terminalia *tomentosa*), bija (*Pterocarpus marsupium*), lendia (*Lagerstroemia parviflora*), haldu (*Haldina cordifolia*), dhaora (*Anogeissus latifolia*), salai (*Boswellia serrata*), aonla (*Emblica officinalis*), amaltas (*Cassia fistula*), gamhar (*Gmelina arborea*), etc. Dazzling white kulu (*Sterculia urens*) trees scattered around stand out conspicuously among the various hues of green. The ground is covered with maze of grasses, plants, bushes and saplings.Pterocarpus marsupium is also used for control of blood sugar in Diabetes since ancient times in India.

Bamboo - Bamboo is also found at places in Madhya Pradesh forests. Normally *Dendrocalamus strictus* is the main bamboo species found overlapping with other species. It is distributed over Balaghat, Seoni, Chhindwara, Betul, Mandla and Shahdol districts.

Khair - Khair (*Acacia catechu*) trees are found in Jabalpur, Sagar, Damoh, Umaria, Hoshangabad, Guna, Shivpuri, Sheopur, Morena, Gwalior etc. Khair trees are used as a raw material for preparation of catechu or kattha.

NWFP - There are many important non-wood forest products (NWFP) found in the forests e.g. tendu leaves or bidi leaves (*Diospyros melonoxylon*), sal seed (*Shorea robusta*), chebulic myrobolan or harra (*Terminalia chebula*), gum, chironji (*Buchanania lanzan*), flower and seeds of mahua (*Madhuca indica*) and flowers, seeds, bark and roots of various plant species. Tendu leaves, sal seed and gums are nationalised forest produce in Madhya Pradesh whereas the other NWFP are non-nationalised. These non-nationalised NWFP can be collected and traded freely. The collection and trade of nationalised forest produce is regulated by the state.

Medicinal plants - Medicinal trees and plants of various kinds are found in abundance in the forests of Madhya Pradesh. Important ones are: *Aegle marmelos, Azadirachta indica, Bixa orellana, Butea monosperma, Asparagus racemosus, Argemone mexicana,Buchanania lanzan, Aloe barbadensis, Acorus calamus, Cassia tora, Curculigo orchioides, Curcuma longa, Embelia ribes, Clitoria ternatea, Mangifera indica, Cassia fistula,*

Evolvulus alsinoides, Commiphora mukul, Helicteres isora, Holorrhaena antidysenterica, Glycyrrhiza glabra, Woodfordia fruticosa,. Dioscorea spp, Plumbago zeylaniea, Terminalia bellirica, Tamarindus indica, Mucuna pruriens, Pongamia pinnata, Terminalia bellirica, Psoralea corylifolia, Phyllanthus embilica, Ocimum americanum, Rauvolfia serpentina, Tinospora cardifolio, Withania somnifera, Swertia chirayita, Tribulus terrestres, Chlorophytum tuberosum, Cyprus rotundus.

Forest growing stock

The total growing stock (volume of timber / wood) is 50,000,000 m^3 valued worth Rs 2.5 lakh Crores.

Natural areas

Madhya Pradesh is home to 9 National Parks, including Bandhavgarh National Park, Kanha National Park, Satpura National Park, Sanjay National Park, Madhav National Park, Van Vihar National Park, Mandla Plant Fossils National Park, Panna National Park, and Pench National Park, Madhya Pradesh.

There are also a number of natural preserves, including Amarkantak, Patalkot, Bagh Caves, Bhedaghat, Bori Natural Reserve, Ken Gharial, Ghatigaon, Kuno Palpur, Narwar, Chambal, Kukdeshwar, Narsinghgarh, Nora Dehi, Pachmarhi, Panpatha, Shikarganj, and Tamia.

National Parks and their Fauna

There are 9 National Parks and 25 Sanctuaries spread over an area of 10,862 km^2 constituting 11.40% of the total forest area and 3.52% of the geographical area of the state. Efforts are under way to increase the Protected Area network to 15% of the forest or 5% of the geographical.

There is a network of Protected Areas representative of bio-geographical zones. Special efforts have been made towards conservation of highly endangered species in the following National Parks and sanctuaries:

- Kanha, Bandhavgarh, Pench, Panna, and Satpura National Park are managed as project tiger areas.
- Sardarpur sanctuary in Dhar and Sailana are managed for conservation of kharmor or lesser florican.
- Ghatigaon sanctuary is managed for great Indian bustard or Son Chiriya.
- National Chambal Sanctuary is managed for conservation of gharial and crocodile, river dolphin, smooth-coated otter and a number of turtle species.
- Ken-gharial and Son-gharial sanctuaries are managed for conservation of gharial and mugger.
- Barasingha is the state animal and dudhraj is the state bird of Madhya Pradesh.

List of sanctuaries

There are 25 Wildlife sanctuaries in Madhya Pradesh. They are the following:

- Bori Wildlife Sanctuary (Hoshangabad) 518.00 km^2 (200.00 sq mi)
- Bagdara Sanctuary (Sidhi) 478.90 km^2 (184.90 sq mi)
- Phen Sanctuary (Mandla) 110.74 km^2 (42.76 sq mi)
- Ghatigaon Sanctuary (Gwalior) 512.00 km^2 (197.68 sq mi)
- Gandhi Sagar Sanctuary (Mandsaur) 368.62 km^2 (142.32 sq mi)
- Karera Sanctuary (Shivpuri) 202.21 km^2 (78.07 sq mi)
- Ken Ghariyal Sanctuary (Chhatarpur, Panna) 45.00 km^2 (17.37 sq mi)
- Kheoni Sanctuary (Dewas, Sehore) 122.70 km^2 (47.37 sq mi)
- Narsingharh Sanctuary (Rajgarh) 57.19 km^2 (22.08 sq mi)
- National Chambal Sanctuary (Morena) 320.00 km^2 (123.55 sq mi)

- Nauradehi Wildlife Sanctuary (Sagar) 1,194.67 km^2 (461.26 sq mi)
- Pachmarhi Sanctuary (Hoshangabad) 461.85 km^2 (178.32 sq mi)
- Panpatha Sanctuary (Shahdol) 245.84 km^2 (94.92 sq mi)
- Kuno Wildlife Sanctuary (Morena) 345.00 km^2 (133.21 sq mi)
- Pench National Park (Seoni, Chhindwara) 449.39 km^2 (173.51 sq mi)
- Ratapani Sanctuary (Raisen) 823.84 km^2 (318.09 sq mi)
- Sanjay-Dubri Wildlife Sanctuary (Sidhi) 364.69 km^2 (140.81 sq mi)
- Singhori Sanctuary (Raisen) 287.91 km^2 (111.16 sq mi)
- Son Ghariyal Sanctuary (Sidhi) 41.80 km^2 (16.14 sq mi)
- Sardarpur Sanctuary (Dhar) 348.12 km^2 (134.41 sq mi)
- Sailana Sanctuary (Ratlam) 12.96 km^2 (5.00 sq mi)
- Ralamandal wildlife Sanctuary (Indore) 5 km^2 (1.9 sq mi)
- Orchha Sanctuary (Tikamgarh) 46 km^2 (18 sq mi)
- Gangau Sanctuary, (Panna and Chhatarpur) 69 km^2 (27 sq mi)
- Veerangna Durgawati Sanctuary (Damoh)24 km^2 (9.3 sq mi)

Climate

Madhya Pradesh has a subtropical climate. Like most of north India, it has a hot dry summer(April–June) followed by monsoon rains (July–September) and a cool and relatively dry winter. The average rainfall is about 1,370 mm (53.9 in). It decreases from east to west. The south-eastern districts have the heaviest rainfall, some places receiving as much as 2,150 mm (84.6 in), while the western and north-western districts receive 1,000 mm (39.4 in) or less.

DAMS IN MADHYA PRADESH

Bansagar

Bansagar or Banasagar is a multipurpose river valley project on Son River in Madhya Pradesh, India envisaging both irrigation and hydroelectric power generation. The Bansagar Dam across Sone River is being constructed at village Deolond in Shahdol district on Rewa – Shahdol road, at a distance of 51.4 km from Rewa. The project has been named as "Bansagar" after Bana Bhatt, the renowned Sanskrit scholar of 7th century, who is believed to have hailed from this region in India. Bansagar Dam is located at Latitude 24-11-30 N and Longitude 81-17-15 E.

Dam and Reservoir Data

- Catchment area : 18648 km^2
- Dam height : 67 metre
- Dam length : 1020 metre
- Dam type : Masonry/Earthen
- Spillway capacity : 47742 cumec
- Live storage : 5410 hm
- Submergence area : 587.54 km^2
- Population affected : 250000 persons (54686 families)
- Villages submerged : 336
- Year of start : 1978
- Year of completion : 2006

Project Benefits

The water sharing from Bansagar Dam is as under:

- Madhya Pradesh : 2.0 Maf (2467 hm)
- Uttar Pradesh : 1.0 Maf (1233 hm)
- Bihar : 1.0 Maf (1233 hm)

Bansagar will provide irrigation facility over an area of 2,490 km^2 in Madhya Pradesh, 1,500 km^2; in Uttar Pradesh and 940 km^2 in Bihar. It also provides power generation of 425 MW in Madhya Pradesh.

Submergence of Bansagar

The Land under submergence of Bansagar at Full Reservoir Level (F.R.L 341.64 m.) is 587.54 km^2, out of which 40.73 km^2 is forest land, 175.90 km^2 revenue land 1.31 km^2 public land and 369.59 km^2 private land.

Total 336 villages have come under submergence of Bansagar Reservoir out of which 79 villages are fully submerged and rest 257 villages are under partial submergence.

Fully Submerged Villages

All the 79 fully submerged villages in Bansagar have been displaced and lost their geographical existence from the map. Some of historically important villages submerged fully are Ramnagar, Deorajnagar, Baraundha, Markandeya-ghat, Darbar etc. The district wise details of these submerged and lost villages are as under:

Satna District (48 villages)

Amjhori Dakshin, Baikona No.-2, Bela (Near Remar), Bamhauri (Bimhauri), Barauli, Baikona No.-1, Bara, Barsajaha, Bela Tiwari, Banneh, Chhirahai, Deoraj Nagar, Dhol baja, Dala, Daga Kothar, Dighiya Khurd, Garehara, Gurha, Hinauta Khurd (Unumukt), Hinauta Khothar, Itma (Near Deoraj Nagar), Itma (Near Ram Nagar), Jarmani, Jirauha, Kusmaha, Khajura, Khajuri, Kauhara, Kareha bela, Kothar, Karahiya, Kalla Khurd, Kalla Kala, Ladwad No.-1, Ladwad No.-2, Mala Dabar, Mohari Khurd, Patha, Patehari, Poriya, Parariya, Pipari Dakshin, Rimar, Semariha, Semra, Singhpur, Semariya (Sanaga), Tilokawa.

Shahdol District (22 villages)

Bodra, Barundha, Dhanedi Purva, Dhaneda, Dhanedi Pashchim, Dhanedi Vikram, Ghusira, Jamun Darhi, Jhirkona, Kusiara, Karahiya, Karri, Karaundiya Pashchim, Karaundiya Purva, Karaundiya Kothar, Kanbau, Kachhara Tola, Marha, Magaraha, Palwahi, Pahariya, Sonvarsha.

Katni District (6 villages)

Amakola, Doli, Itahara, Kudri, Naubasta, Podi.

Umaria District (3 villages)

Darbar, Sahijana and Hinauti.

Dedicated to Nation

The Bansagar Dam was dedicated to nation on 25 September 2006 by Atal Bihari Vajpayee, former Prime Minister of India. The foundation of ambitious Bansagar project was laid by Late Prime Minister Morarji Desai on 14 May 1978.

BARGI DAM

Bargi Dam is one of the first completed Dam out of the chain of 30 major dams to be constructed on Narmada River in Madhya Pradesh, India. The Narmada is the largest river in Madhya Pradesh, flowing towards the west and falling in the Arabian Sea. Its total length is 1312 km of which it covers 1072 km in Madhya Pradesh. The Central Water and Power Commission conceptualized the proposal of this dam construction in 1968 envisaging irrigation in 2,980 square kilometres and hydropower generation capacity of 105 MW. (Source: DPR, Govt of M.P. 1968). Later the Bargi diversion scheme was planned, increasing the total irrigation potential to 4,370 square kilometres. The dam construction work started in 1974 and was completed in 1990 when the dam was filled to its complete capacity. The height of the dam is 69 m and length 5.4 km. A lake of about 75 km in length and 4.5 km width, spreading over 267.97 km^2. In Jabalpur, Mandla and Seoni districts is formed when the water is impounded up to the dam FRL of 422.76 m.

Gandhi Sagar Dam

The Gandhi Sagar dam is the first of the four dams built on the Chambal river. It is located in the Mandsaur district of Madhya Pradesh. It is a 64 metre high masonry gravity dam, with a live storage capacity of 6,920 Mm^3 and a catchment area of 22,584 km^2. The dam was completed in the year 1960. The hydro-power station comprises five generating units, four of 23 MW each and one 27 MW capacity. The water released after power generation is utilised for irrigation through Kota Barrage.

Rajghat

Rajghat is an Inter-state Dam project of the Government of Madhya Pradesh and Uttar Pradesh being constructed on Betwa River about 22 km from Lalitpur in Uttar Pradesh, India. The project envisages construction of 43.80 m high and 562.50 m long masonry dam across River Betwa flanked by an earthen dam having maximum height of 29.5 m and a total length of 10.79 km.

The project will provide irrigation to 1,380 square kilometres of land in Uttar Pradesh and 1,210 square kilometres in Madhya Pradesh. The installed capacity of the power house is 45 MW (3 x 15 MW). The costs and benefits of the project are to be shared by these two States equally.

The projects existing on the downstream are Matatila Dam Project, Dhukwan and Parichha Weirs. Thus, the Rajghat Dam Project will serve as mother storage for Irrigation in Uttar Pradesh and Madhya Pradesh through a cascade of hydraulic structures in the downstream of River Betwa.

Tawa Reservoir

Tawa Reservoir is a large reservoir on the Tawa River in central India. It is located in Hoshangabad District of Madhya Pradesh state. The reservoir was formed by the construction of the Tawa Dam, which began in 1958 and was completed in 1978. forty-four villages were submerged by the reservoir.

Tawa Reservoir forms the western boundary of Satpura National Park and Bori Wildlife Sanctuary. (2001 est. pop. 60.4 million). Madhya Pradesh is a central Indian state (named from a Hindi translation of the old British unit called Central Provinces). It is entirely landlocked, being bounded on the south by Maharashtra, on the east by Chhattisgarh, on the north by Uttar Pradesh and on the west by Gujarat. It is virtually bisected from east to west by the Narmada River. The state was formed in 1956, and its reduced area was 273,994 square kilometres in 2000, when the eastern third of the state was sliced off to create Chhattisgarh state.

The landscape consists of forested hills with extensive plateaus and steep slopes. The Vindhya and the Satpura Ranges cover much of the northern and southern parts of the state, respectively. The capital is Bhopal (2001 est. pop. 1.4 million), though the largest city is Indore (2001 est. pop. 1.6 million). Although there are numerous towns, three-quarters of the inhabitants are rural.

The greatest disaster in modern times in this state was the deadly gas leak on 3 December 1984, at the Union Carbide plant in Bhopal. This killed some 2,500 residents and injured another 2,000. Most survivors have received virtually no compensation.

Madhya Pradesh was a part of the Mauryan Empire in the fourth to third centuries BCE. Later it was a part of Harsha's Empire (seventh century, and then of the Delhi Sultanate (eleventh century). In 1527 the Mughal empire extended into this area when Babur conquered Chanderi; and in the later seventeenth century, a Bhopal State was formed when the Afghan chief Dost Muhammad conquered the area. In 1817 this was annexed by the East India Company, and was administered by the British until 1947.

Cultivated crops include cotton, rice, wheat, pulses, linseed and other oilseeds, castor, soybean, millet, mustard and tobacco. The diverse industries are located mostly in the western half of the state, and include electronics, aluminum, rayon, fertilizer, petrochemicals, paper, tires and tubes, industrial gases, and cables. But the state is primarily agrarian, with low productivity.

Land use in 1991 was 43.2 percent agriculture, 30.7 percent forest, and 26.1 percent other purposes. Some 93 percent of the population are Hindus, and 86 percent speak Hindi as their first language. Tourist sites of outstanding historical importance include Sanchi, Ujjain, Gwalior, Indore, and Bhopal. The state has 448 colleges but no university of major stature.

Madhya Pradesh pronunciation (help info), IPA:/madhjy pryde) is a state in central India. Its capital is Bhopal. Madhya Pradesh was originally the largest state in India until November 1, 2000 when the state of Chhattisgarh was carved out. It borders the states Uttar Pradesh, Chhattisgarh, Maharashtra, Gujarat and Rajasthan.

Origin of Name

This state is in the centre of the nation and therefore it is called Madhya Pradesh, *meaning "central state".*

THE FORESTS

Forest Area: Madhya Pradesh is endowed with rich and diverse forest resources. Lying between lat. 21°04'N and long. 74°02' and 82°49' E, it is a reservoir of biodiversity. The geographical area of the state is 3,08,144 km^2 which constitutes 9.38% of the land area of the country. The forest area of the state is 95,221 km^2 constituting 31% of the geographical area of the state and 12.44% of the forest area of the country. Legally this area has been classified into "Reserved Forest, Protected Forest and Unclassified Forest", which constitute 61.7%, 37.4% and 0.9% of the forest area respectively. Per capita forest area is 2,100 m^2 as against the national average of 700 m^2.

Forest Composition: Central, eastern and southern parts of the state are rich, whereas northern and western parts are deficient in forest. Variability in climatic and edaphic conditions brings about significant difference in the forest types of the state. There are four important forest types *viz.* Tropical Moist, Tropical Dry, Tropical Thorn, Subtropical broadleaved Hill forests. The forest area can also be classified based on the composition of forest and terrain of the area.

Based on composition, there are three important forest formations namely Teak forest, Sal forest and Miscellaneous Forests. Bamboo bearing areas are widely distributed in the state. To obviate pressure on the natural forests, plantations have been undertaken in forest and non forest areas to supplement the availability of fuel wood, small timber, fodder etc.

Forest Growing Stock: The total growing stock (volume of timber / wood) is 500 lakh m^3 valued worth Rs 2.5 lakh Crores.

WILD LIFE

National Parks

No.	*Name*
1.	Kanha
2.	Bandhavgarh
3.	Panna
4.	Pench
5.	Satpura
6.	Sanjay
7.	Madhav
8.	Vanvihar
9.	Fossil

Sanctuaries

1. Bori
2. Bagdara
3. Phen
4. Ghatigaon
5. Gandhisagar
6. Karera
7. Ken Ghariyal
8. Kheoni
9. Narsinghgarh
10. N. Chambal
11. Nauradehi
12. Pachmari

13. Panpatha
14. Kuno
15. Pench
16. Ratapani
17. Sanjay Dubri
18. Singhori
19. Son Ghariyal
20. Sardapur
21. Sailana
22. Ralamandal
23. Orchha
24. Gangau
25. V. Durgawati

In-situ Conservation Areas

- *National Parks and Sancturies:* Madhya Pradesh is a pioneer state in the national movement for conservation of flora and fauna. Conservation oriented legal proviso were made in the erstwhile Acts regulating hunting of game -birds and wild animals. In tune with the national consciousness towards conservation of flora and fauna the state government began setting up a network of in-situ conservation areas (national parks and sanctuaries) under the provisions of the Wildlife (Protection) Act, 1972. There are 9 National Parks and 25 Sanctuaries spread over an area of 10,862 sq. km constituting 11.40% of the total forest area and 3.52% of the geographical area of the state. Efforts are under way to increase the Protected Area network to 15% of the forest or 5% of the geographical area as suggested by State Wildlife Board.
- *Project Tiger Areas*: Government of India/WWF launched "Project Tiger" in the year 1973. Kanha National Park was one of the first nine Protected Areas selected under Project Tiger in the country. At present, there are 5 Project

Tiger areas in the state namely – Kanha, Panna, Bandhavgarh, Pench and Satpura. Madhya Pradesh is also known as the 'Tiger State' as it harbours 19% of India's Tiger Population and 10% of the world's tiger population.

Ex-Situ Conservation Area

Van Vihar National Park, Bhopal is the only Ex-Situ conservation area that has been given provisional recognition by the Central Zoo Authority (CZA).

Though, this area has been notified as a National Park in order to provide adequate legal protection, it is being managed as a modern zoological park. Here the captive wild animals have been kept in near natural habitat setup.

Wildlife Wing

The wildlife wing is headed by the Chief Wildlife Warden and Principal Chief Conservator of Forests (Wildlife) to oversee implementation of policies and programmes for Wildlife conservation and management in the state.

Objectives

- To Conserve Wildlife and biodiversity through a network of protected areas and ex-situ conservation areas
- To take up special measures for protection and conservation of highly endangered spp.
- To curb poaching and illicit trade in wildlife and wildlife parts and articles
- Sustainable development of forest fringe villages through participatory planning and implementation of eco-development in and around Protected Areas
- To elicit public support for conservation of wildlife and wild habitats through conservation awareness programmes and ecotourism.

Strategy for Wildlife Conservation

Establishment of a Protected Area Network: Conservation of wild habitats and wildlife through establishment of a network of Protected Areas representative of bio-geographical zones has been the prime strategy of the government. Special efforts have been made towards conservation of highly endangered spp.

1. Kanha, Bandhavgarh, Pench, Panna, and Satpura national park are managed as project tiger areas.
2. Sardar pur sanctuary in Dhar and Sailana are managed for conservation of kharmor or lesser florican.
3. Ghatigaon sanctuary is managed for great Indian bustard or Son Chiriya.
4. National Chambal sanctuary is managed for conservation of gharial and mugger, River dolphin, smooth coated otter and a number of turtle species.
5. Ken -gharial and Son-gharial sanctuaries are managed for conservation of gharial and mugger.

   Management Planning: For scientific management of PAs, Management Plans have been prepared. In some areas, plans are under various stages of completion or revision. The basic difference between forest Working Plan and Protected Area Management in India lies in their objectives. While working plan is based on the principle of sustainable harvesting of forest resources and increasing productivity of forests, a PA Management Plan includes prescriptions for non-consumptive management of crucial habitat units such as –Food, Water and Cover and aims at maintaining diversity of species and habitats in order to maintain ecological processes and functions Management Interventions.

Ameliorative and Compensatory Management

Wildlife management includes both ameliorative and compensatory management. Certain important aspects of wildlife management are:

- Improvement of habitat that includes augmenting water sources, water regime development, eradication of weeds, and development and restoration of grasslands,

- Development of communication and protection infrastructure,
- Patrolling and anti-poaching activities,
- Research and monitoring,
- Mitigation of man-animal conflicts,
- Innoculation of domestic cattle in and around PAs against contagious diseases,
- visitor-use management (tourism) and interpretation,
- Maintenance of roads, check-barriers, patrolling camps, buildings, watch towers, wireless network, water sources, vehicles etc. are part of the day to day management activity.

Ecodevelopent

Ecodevelopment means 'development' that is **ecologically, socially** and **economically** sustainable. It is initiated through site-specific village level planning by villagers themselves to achieve sustainable development of village resources, alternatives to fuel, fodder and timber and schemes to provide job alternatives to individuals and families in order to eradicate forest dependent livelihood patterns and ensure people's active participation in protection of PA resources. The ecodevelopment activities are being executed through participatory management since 1992-93. Till 1995, only the central government has been funding the ecodevelopment programmes in the villages around PAs. This programme was strengthened by the international funding through the MP Forestry Project (a World Bank Aided project) and India Ecodevelopment Project (a World Bank And Global Environmental Trust aided project).

About 700 ecodevelopment committees have been constituted in and around protected areas in M.P.At present ecodevelopment activities are being carried out with 100%financial assistance from the central government under the Project Tiger Scheme and Development of National Parks and Sanctuaries Scheme.

Voluntary Village Relocation Activity: In order to

safeguard the precious gene pool of flora and fauna, biotic interference from the existing village needs to be removed. Village relocation from remote forest areas also benefits the villagers as they get an opportunity to reap the benefits of mainstream development at the relocation site. Village relocation programme is being implemented in some PAs where people have agreed for relocation to some suitable site outside the PA. GoI is funding the Village Relocation Scheme. Respective Collectors of the district are carrying out the settlement process under the Wildlife (Protection Act) and the PA managers are doing the relocation work.

Status of Relocation of Villages from PAs

Protected Area	*No. of Villages inside at the beginning*		*No. of Relocated Villages*	*Relocation still in Progress*	*Relocation proposals submitted*
	Revenue	*Forest*			
Panna	16	0	3	8	2
Madhav	15	0	0	1	1
Satpura	38	26	0	1	12
Bandhavgarh	3	3	0	0	4
Kanha	0	45	27	0	1
Kuno	24	0	24	12 (out of 24)	0
Pench	0	0	2	0	0
Sanjay	18	0	1		

As a matter of policy, no forced relocation is permitted. The whole process of relocation is totally participatory. No village is to be relocated if the inhabitants are unwilling to move. As per norms made by Government of India, an amount of Rs. 1 lakh is spent on the relocation of each family. Government of India has been urged to revise the village relocation-funding norm from Rs 1 Lakh to at least Rs 2 lakh per family. The works include development of land at the relocation site, development of potable as well as irrigation water facility, roads and housing, pasture and fuel-wood plantation, transportation of household goods to the site of relocation etc.

Compensation for Damage Caused by Wild Animals: The State Government provides compensation for the loss of human life by tiger, leopard, wolf, bear, elephant, wild pig, gaur and hyena.

A compensation of Rs 50,000 is paid to the successor of the deceased person, and on being injured by wild animals compensation up to Rs 10,000 is paid towards treatment, in case of permanent disability compensation up to Rs. 37500. may be paid to the injured person. In case of loss of domestic animals, compensation up to Rs 5000 is paid. To facilitate expeditious payment of compensation to people range officers are authorized to investigate and make payment within a timeframe.

Monitoring—Population Estimation of Wild Animals: In all the National Parks and Wildlife Sanctuaries and also territorial divisions, population estimation of major herbivorous and carnivorous wild animals is done annually. As per the population estimates of 2003, there are 712 tigers and 1,090 Panthers in the State.

The Forest Department solicits the voluntary participation of college students and NGOs in training and actual estimation work in the field. Annual Tiger/Panther and Wild Animal Population Estimation Technical and Administrative Manual, incorporating project tiger guidelines was issued by the Chief Wild Life Warden of the state wherein the entire procedure and techniques of wild animal population estimation are codified.

In 2005 the Central Government initiated Nationwide Population estimation exercise based on an entirely new methodology developed by WII, Dehradun. The exercise began in December2005 and a series of trainings were organised in all the PAs and Forest Divisions of M.P followed by a massive data collection and February 2006. The work related to compilation of data is complete and the data have been sent to WII for analysis.

Training of Personnel and Members of Eco Development Committees: The Deputy Conservators and Astt. Conservators are trained in Wildlife Management, a 9 month PG Diploma course at Wildlife Institute of India(WII), Dehradun. The WII organises a Certificate course for Range Officers. For training of Guards, the Forest Department has established a Biodiversity Training Centre at Bandhavgarh National Park. Since October, 1998 a new 6- month curriculum, designed to impart competence based training, is being implemented. Several short-term modules are also conducted for field personnel at various levels of hierarchy. Motivational and skill trainings and study tours are conducted by the PAs for members of EDCs.

State Board for Wildlife: The State Government has constituted the State Wildlife Advisory Board renamed State Board for Wildlife as provided in Section-6 of the Wildlife (Protection) amendment Act, 2002. This is a statutory body under Wildlife (protection) Act,1972. The Board meets twice yearly to advise the State Government on wildlife conservation matters. The Hon'ble Chief minister of Madhya Pradesh is the Chairperson of the Board and Hon'ble Forest minister is the Vice Chairperson, the Chief Wildlife Warden, M.P. is the member secretary.

Funding Mechanism

State and Central Schemes: The GoI provides Central Assistance for wildlife habitat improvement, protection from fire and destruction, poaching control measures, and development of infrastructure such as roads and buildings and establishment of wireless network in all the 34 Protected Areas of the State under following schemes-

Two Earlier Schemes: 'The Ecodevelopment Shceme' and the 'Beneficiary oriented Tribal Development schemes' for relocation of Villages have been merged with the Project Tiger and Development of Parks and Sanctuaries Schemes since 1999.

Recurring annual expenditure and Establishment of all the PA's is met from state budget under two head (1) Non-plan (2) Plan. Average allotments under each head per annum have been 1200 lakhs and 1300 lakhs respectively till 2002-03. Since 2003 the central government has enhanced allocation under central schemes. At present the state receives around Rs 1600-1700 lakhs as central assistance for protected areas. Including the central assistance and non-plan allocation (of which around 60 % is spent on salaries) on an average, the Wildlife wing in the State gets an allotment to the tune of 3400 lakhs per annum. This leaves a deficit of Rs. 3300 lakhs per annum.

RIVERS

The Narmada is the longest river in Madhya Pradesh. It flows westward through a rift valley, with the Vindhya ranges sprawling along its northern bank and the Satpura range of mountains along the southern. Its tributaries include the Banjar, the Tawa, the Machna, the Shakkar, the Denwa and the Sonbhadra rivers. The Tapti River runs parallel to Narmada, and also flows through a rift valley. The Narmada–Tapti systems carry an enormous volume of water and provide drainage for almost a quarter of the land area of Madhya Pradesh. The Narmada river is considered very sacred and is worshipped throughout the region. It is the main source of water and acts as a lifeline to the state.

The Vindhyas form the southern boundary of the Ganges basin, with the western part of the Ganges basin draining into the Yamuna and the eastern part directly into the Ganges itself. All the rivers, which drain into the Ganges, flow from south to north, with the Chambal, Shipra, Kali Sindh, Parbati, Kuno, Sind, Betwa, Dhasan and Ken rivers being the main tributaries of the Yamuna. Shipra River is one of the most sacred rivers of Hinduism. It is the site of the Simhastha Kumbh Mela, which is held every 12 years. The land drained by these rivers is agriculturally rich, with the natural vegetation largely consisting of grass and dry deciduous forest types, largely thorny. The eastern part of the Ganges basin consists of the Son, the Tons and the Rihand Rivers. Son, which arises in the Maikal hills around Amarkantak, is the largest tributary that goes into the Ganges on the south bank and that does not arise from the Himalayas. Son and its tributaries contribute the bulk of the monsoon flow into the Ganges, because the north bank tributaries are all snow fed. The forests in their basins are much richer than the thorn forests of the northwestern part of Madhya Pradesh.

After the formation of Chhattisgarh State, the major portion of Mahanadi basin now lies in Chhattisgarh. Presently, only 154 km^2 basin area of Hasdeo River in Anuppur District lies in Madhya Pradesh.

The Satpuras, in the Gawilgarh and Mahadeo Hills, also contain a watershed, which is south facing. The Wainganga, the Wardha, the Pench, the Kanhan rivers, discharge an enormous volume of water into the Godavari river system. The Godavari basin consists of sub-tropical, semi-moist forests, mainly in the valley of the Indrawati. There are many important multi-state irrigation projects in development, including the Godavari River Basin Irrigation Projects.

Madhya Pradesh represents great river basins and the watershed of a number of rivers. Catchments of many rivers of India are lying in Madhya Pradesh. The Narmada and Tapti rivers and their basins divide the state in two, with the northern part draining largely into the Ganga basin and the southern part into the Godavari and Mahanadi systems. The Vindhyas form the southern boundary of the Ganga basin, with the western part of the Ganga basin draining into the Yamuna and the eastern part directly into the Ganga itself.

All the rivers, which drain into the Ganga, flow from south to north, with the Chambal, Sipra, Kali Sind, Parbati, Kuno, Sind, Betwa, Dhasan and Ken rivers being the main tributaries of the Yamuna. The land drained by these rivers is agriculturally rich, with the natural vegetation largely consisting of grass and dry deciduous forest types, largely thorny. The eastern part of the Ganga basin consists of the Son, the Tons and the Rihand Rivers, with the Son being the major tributary. This is also the junction point of the Satpura and the Vindhya ranges, with the Maikal and Kaimur Hills being the fulcrum.

The forests here are much richer than the thorn forests of the northwestern part of Madhya Pradesh. The Son is of great significance in that it is the largest tributary going into the Ganga on the south bank and arising out of the hills of Madhya Pradesh rather than from the Himalayas. This river and its tributaries contribute the bulk of the monsoon flow into Ganga, because the north bank tributaries are all snow fed.

The major tributary of the Ganga, the Son, arises in one of the most important watersheds in India, the Maikal hills around Amarkantak. Three of the great rivers of India, Narmada, Mahanadi and Son, are given birth to by these hills. This is also one of the few ranges in the State having a north south configuration.

The Mahanadi itself, together with its tributaries such as Hasdeo, Mand and Kharun flows southeast into Orissa and converts that State into a green rice bowl. The upper Mahanadi catchment contains some of the finest forests in the State, ranging from mixed deciduous to teak, bamboo and Sal. Just as the Mahanadi flows east from the Maikal hills and the Son flows north, the mighty Narmada charts a westerly course from these very hills. The Narmada flows through a rift valley, with the Vindhyas marching along its northern bank and the Satpuras along the southern.

Its tributaries include the Banjar, the Tawa, the Machna, the Denwa and the Sonbhardra rivers. Taken in combination with its parallel sister river, the Tapti, which also flows through a rift valley, the Narmada - Tapti systems carry and enormous volume of water and provide drainage for almost a quarter of the land area of Madhya Pradesh.

The Satpuras, in the Gawligarh and Mahadeo Hills, also contain a watershed, which is south facing. The Indrawati, the Wainganga, the Wardha, the Pench, the Kanhan and Penganga rivers, discharge an enormous volume of water into the Godavari system. The Godavari is the lifeline of Andhra Pradesh, but the water which feeds it is a gift of the Central India watershed.

Some of the finest sub-tropical, semi moist forests in India are to be found in the Godavari basin, mainly in the valley of the Indrawati. There are very few virgin forests left in the country, but very fine examples of these are to be found in Bastar area along the Indrawati and in the Kanger valley in Chhattisgarh.

The importance of Central India watershed was first noted by Captain Forsyth and remarked upon in his book, "The Highlands of Central India", first published in 1889. This is what he has to state in the introductory chapter to his book, "Yet in the very centre of India there exists a considerable region to which the term highlands—is strictly applicable; and in which are enormous peaks and ranges, for which the term mountain would, in any other country, be used.

Several of the great rivers of India have their first source in this elevated region. And pour their water into the sea on either side of the peninsula – to the north the Son comingling with the Ganges, to the east the Mahanadi, flowing independently to the Bay of Bengal, to the south some of the principal feeders of the Godavari, and to the west the Narmada and the Tapti taking parallel courses to the Arabian Sea."

Regions

Madhya Pradesh is divided into the following agro-climatic zones:

- Kaimur Plateau and Satpura Hills
- Vindhyan Plateau (Hills)
- Narmada valley
- Wainganga valley
- Gird (Gwalior) Region
- Bundelkhand Region

- Satpura Plateau (Hills)
- Malwa Plateau
- Nimar Plateau
- Jhabua Hills
- Leeshiv
- Gidaila

Administratation

Madhya Pradesh is administratively divided into 10 divisions and further 52 districts.

- Bhopal Division
- Chambal Division
- Gwalior Division
- Indore Division
- Jabalpur Division
- Narmadapuram Division
- Rewa Division
- Sagar Division
- Shahdol Division
- Ujjain Division

6

Economy

INTRODUCTION

The economy of Madhya Pradesh grew at 12% GDP for annual year 2011–12. Madhya Pradesh received an award from President Pranab Mukharjee in January 2013 for improving its tourism, medical and infrastructural growth.

Madhya Pradesh's gross state domestic product (nominal GDP) for 2013-14 was 4,509 billion (approximately US$ 72,726,000,000). The per-capita figure was US$ 871.45 in 2013-14, the sixth-lowest in the country. Between 1999 and 2008, the annualised growth rate of the state was very low: 3.5%. Subsequently, the state's GDP growth rate has improved significantly, rising to 8% during 2010–11 and 12% during 2011–12.

Madhya pradesh is also famous for honey production in district Morena.

The state has an agrarian economy. The major crops of Madhya Pradesh are wheat, soybean, gram, sugarcane, rice, maize, cotton, rapeseed, mustard and arhar. Minor Forest Produce (MFP), such as tendu leaves used to roll beedi, sal seed, teak seed, and lak also contribute to state's rural economy.

Madhya Pradesh has 5 Special Economic Zones (SEZs):

3 IT/ITeS (Indore, Gwalior), 1 mineral-based (Jabalpur) and 1 agro-based (Jabalpur). In October 2011, approval was given to 14 proposed SEZs, out of which 10 were IT/ITeS-based.

Indore is the major commercial centre of the state. Because of the state's central location, a number of consumer goods companies have established manufacturing bases in MP.

The state has the largest reserves of diamond and copper in India. Other major mineral reserves include those of coal, coalbed methane, manganese and dolomite.

Madhya Pradesh has six Ordnance Factories, four of which are located at Jabalpur (Vehicle Factory, Grey Iron Foundry, Gun Carriage Factory, Ordnance Factory Khamaria) and one each at Katni and Itarsi.

The factories are run by the Ordnance Factories Board, and manufacture a variety of products for the Indian Armed Forces.

Madhya Pradesh won the 10th National Award for excellent work in Mahatma Gandhi National Rural Employment Guarantee Act, 2005.

The state's tourism industry is growing, fuelled by wildlife tourism and a number of places of historical and religious significance.

Sanchi and Khajuraho are frequented by external tourists. Besides the major cities, Bhedaghat, Bhimbetka, Bhojpur, Maheshwar, Mandu, Orchha, Pachmarhi, Kanha, Jabalpur and Ujjain, Tumen Vindhyavasini temple ancient temple.

This south facing Ashok Nagar district located in Tuman (Tumvn). Yho digging in the release of the ancient statues it is known as the city of Raja Mordwaj Yho Vlram temple in ancient Dashnik destinations, Hazarmuki Mahadev Mandir, Triveni Sangam, Voddh statues, Lakhavnjara Wakr, caves etc. popular are the other popular tourist destinations.

Macro-economic trend

Following is a table showing trend of gross state domestic product of Madhya Pradesh at market prices estimated by

Ministry of Statistics and Programme Implementation with figures in millions of Indian Rupees.

Year	Gross State Domestic Product
1980	77,880
1985	139,050
1990	304,720
1995	478,410
2000	737,150
2005	1,044,850

After partition, the new Madhya Pradesh state produces about 70% of the output of the old Madhya Pradesh state – the rest is produced by Chhattisgarh. The state's debt was estimated at 51 per cent of its GDP by 2005.

Agriculture

Woman harvesting wheat, Raisen district

This is a chart of output of major commodities of Madhya Pradesh.

Commodity	National Share
Soybeans	90%
Grams	36%
Oilseeds	25%
Pulses	24%
Food grains	8%

Industry

Until 2005, there was only one *S&P CNX 500* conglomerate with its corporate office in Madhya Pradesh *viz.* Ruchi Soya Industries (2005 gross income Rs 49,661 million). Now there are many big industries having their base in the state. State-run NTPC will invest about Rs 20,000 crore to set up a 3,960-megawatt (Mw) coal-based power project in Madhya Pradesh. NTPC had signed a memorandum of understanding with the state government and MP Power Trading Company regarding this

Madhya Pradesh has 6 Ordnance Factories, 4 of which are located at Jabalpur (Vehicle Factory, Grey Iron Foundry, Gun Carriage Factory, Ordnance Factory Khamaria) and one each at Katni and Itarsi. The factories are run by the Ordnance Factories Board, and manufacture a variety of products for the Indian Armed Forces.

Minor forest produce

MFP from the forests, such as Tendu leaves used to roll bidis, sal seed, teak seed and lak are a major contributor to the rural economy of the state. MFP-PARC (Minor Forest Produce - Processing & Research Centre) is located in the state capital - Bhopal. MFP-PARC is a unit of M P Minor Forest Produce (Trading & Development) Co-operative Federation Limited. "Vindhya Herbals" is the brand of various ayurvedic, herbal & fruit products produced by M P MFP Federation. Apart from MFP-PARC, these products are also produced in Rehti (Sehore District), Barman (Narsinghpur District), Katni, Panna & Dewas in Madhya Pradesh. Some more processing centres are in the pipeline.

Economy of main districts

Bhopal

Bhopal is the capital and the second largest city in the state and largest city in terms of area. Initially the economic growth stalled because of the Bhopal Gas Tragedy but now has started growing again. Its economy is mainly based on Industries. It is an important Industrial center of the state. Electrical goods, cotton, chemicals and flour milling are the main source of economy. Zardaori and embroidery of Bhopal's old city is also famous. The district is highly urbanised with nearly 80% of the population marked as urban. Now being a metropolitan city, many Software/IT sectors companies are setting up offices in the city. Bhopal is also an important tourist place with the following destinations near the city:

- Islamnagar (11 km away): Palace built by the Bhopal's Afghan rulers
- Bhimbetka rock shelters (45 km away): Archeological site of the Paleolithic era. A UNESCO World Heritage Site
- Sanchi Stupa (46 km away): A Buddhist Stupa commissioned by the emperor Ashoka the Great in the 3rd century BC

GDP ($US) : 20 Billion

Gwalior

Gwalior enjoys being at a very strategic position as being a main junction on New Delhi - Chennai railroad and being on NH-3 and NH-75. Gwalior is surrounded by 3 Industrial areas - Sitholi, Banmore and Malanpur. All these three sectors are on NH 75, National Highway 3 and NH 92 respectively. Malanpur is the biggest. The city earlier had big manufacturing industries such as Gwalior Grasim and J.C. MILLS of Birlanagar but now this sector is left with only one industry – J.B.Mangharam Ltd. But the other three sectors have many industries. The important ones are dairy, chemical, manufacturing, and textiles. Handicraft and small industries are also found such as Gwalior potteries. Gwalior is also an important historical and tourism sector of the country therefore tourism sector also puts an effect into the city's economy. Gwalior trade fair is an annual trade fair showcasing economy of Gwalior.

GDP ($US) : 15 billion

Indore

Indore is commercial capital of Madhya Pradesh with a bulk of its trade coming from large, medium and small scale manufacturing and service industries. These industries range from Automobile to Pharmaceutical and from Software to Retail and from Textile trading to Real estate. Major industrial areas surrounding the city include the Pithampur Special Economic Zone and the Sanwer Industrial belt.

While the Textile manufacturing and Trading is the oldest business to contribute to economy, the Real Estate has emerged very fast in past few years. National Real Estate Players DLF Limited,Omaxe,Sahara, Parsvnath, Ansal API, Emaar MGF have already launched their residential projects in Indore.

These projects are generally on the Indore bypass.This road also houses the projects of many local and regional Real estate players like Silver spring, Kalindi, Milan Heights etc. Major software firms in Indore include Worldpay ,Impetus, IBM India and Computer Sciences Corporation (CSC).

Also many small and medium size software development firms are also established. In the software front a major event occurred in the first half of 2011 when India's biggest software company Tata Consultancy Services decided to open a campus in Indore.

Government of MP has also done the land allotment. Infosys, country's second largest information technology services company, plans to set up new development centre at Indore at an investment of Rs 100 crore in phase one. Pithampur near Indore houses production plants of various Pharmaceutical companies like Ipca Laboratories, Cipla, Lupin, Glenmark, Unichem.

GDP ($US) : 25 billion

Jabalpur

The Narmada river bringing in fresh water from the Vindyachal Ranges has developed Jabalpur district into an agrarian economy. The land of the Narmada basin with its fertile alluvial soil gives good yields of sorghum, wheat, rice and millet in the villages around Jabalpur. Important among commercial crops are pulses, oilseeds, cotton, sugar cane and medicinal crops.

The state is poised for a breakthrough in soybean cultivation. In Kharif crops occupy 60% and Rabi crops 40% area with 71.4% area under food grain production. Nearly 59% of landholders are marginal whereas small farmed share 18% of farmland.

Low literacy rates (35.45%), undulating topography, high percentages of waste land (13.2%), underdeveloped irrigation potential (23%), low ground water utilization, large proportion of rain fed agriculture (75%), practice of Kharif fallows (3.6%), low cropping intensity (131%), low fertilizer consumption (50 kg/ha), high proportion of low value crops, and high numbers of unproductive livestock constrain production in the state. Jabalpur has a variety of industries largely based in mineral substances of economic value found in the district, although the ready-made garments industry is a substantial portion of production in Jabalpur. Defence establishments started in the early 20th century.

Jabalpur has Vehicle Factory Jabalpur, Grey Iron Foundry, Gun Carriage Factory Jabalpur and Ordnance Factory Khamaria which belong to the Ordnance Factories Board manufacturing various products for the Indian Armed Forces. The Gun Carriage Factory was started in the year 1904 is well equipped and manufacture gun parts, mounting, shells and a variety of the other product for war purpose. Vehicle Factory

Jabalpur (VFJ) was started as manufacturer of trucks and other defence vehicles. Other two are Grey Iron Foundry (GIF) and Ordnance Factory Khamaria (OFK).

Armed forces make up a large portion of the city and economy in this city. The city has three regimental centres: Grenadiers, Jammu and Kashmir rifles and the Signals regiment.

Jabalpur is also the army headquarters of Madhya Pradesh, Bihar, Chhattisgarh, and Orissa. Jabalpur is an important divisional headquarters, having eight districts: Jabalpur, Seoni, Mandla, Chhindwara, Narsimhapur, Katni, Dindori, Balaghat. The Jabalpur District has been reconstituted on May 25, 1998. It now has four tehsils Jabalpur, Sihora, Patan and Kundam. Jabalpur also has the headquarters of the Madhya Pradesh State Electricity Board, Homeguards and many other state and central government offices. There are seven blocks in the district with 1449 inhabited villages, 60 uninhabited, 1209 revenue villages and 4 forest villages. The presence of several industries in Jabalpur bolstered the industrial scenario of the city. However the industrial growth of the area owes much to the defense establishments and the four ordnance factories. The presence of the military base and the ordnance factories have improved the infrastructure of the city. This has boosted the industrial development of Jabalpur. The important industries in Jabalpur are:

- Readymade garments units
- Poultry/hatchery
- Electrical goods industry
- Sawmills
- Wood cutting industry
- Industries relating to lime stone products
- Building materials
- Glassware
- Telephone parts
- Furniture making industry
- Shaw Wallace Gelatin Factory

- Steel structures works
- Cement industries
- Commercial Engineers & Body Builders Co Limited [CEBBCO]
- Tobacco business
- Retail busine
- Food processing industry
- Vendors for Coca-Cola India & Parle

GDP ($US) : 9.7 billion

Ujjain

Ujjain is the largest city in Ujjain district of the Indian state of Madhya Pradesh. It is the fifth largest city in Madhya Pradesh by population and is the administrative centre of Ujjain district and Ujjain division.

An ancient city situated on the eastern bank of the Kshipra River, Ujjain was the most prominent city on the Malwa plateau of central India for much of its history. It emerged as the political centre of central India around 600 BCE. It was the capital of the ancient Avanti kingdom, one of the sixteen mahajanapadas. It remained an important political, commercial and cultural centre of central India until the early 19th century, when the British administrators decided to develop Indore as an alternative to it. Ujjain continues to be an important place of pilgrimage for Shaivites, Vaishnavites and followers of Shakta.

Ujjain has been selected as one of the hundred Indian cities to be developed as a smart city under PM Narendra Modi's flagship Smart Cities Mission. GDP ($US) : 2.9 billion

Dewas

In the recent years, modern industry has taken off in Dewas in a big way. The growth is industry sector has given jobs to local factories. At the same time, traditional crafts / Handicrafts as Mojri (Shoes), Synthetic Carpets, leather works (begs, belts, ladies purses, shoes, coats, briefcases etc.) remain important in the economy. Agriculture (specially Soybean, wheat, gram) is also the source of economy. Many high tech industries have been set up for oil extraction from Soyabean. To control the Indian economy, BANK NOTE PRESS, a Central Government Organization for printing of Indian Currency is also situated here. GDP ($US) : 5.4 billion

Ratlam

The city of Ratlam located in northwestern part of the state of Madhya Pradesh since long has been known for its economic and commercial activities . The region which was once famous for its opium and tobacco trade has grown in its size and proportion. With agricultural background this city this is one of the most productive region of the state. In last two decades many small and medium-sized Agro- based industries has made appearances on the canvas of Ratlam. These industries have acted as generator of employment transforming the lives of peoples in Ratlam. The city is also home to many chemical factories namely IPCA, JVL, Hightech, Shaba Chemicals, Bordiya Chemicals, Sujjan Chemicals etc. GDP ($US) : 4.1 billion

Rewa

Rewa district is particularly rich in mineral resources as a large variety of important minerals are found here. Limestone, Sandstone, industrial minerals like phosphate, asbestos, calcite, Talc (soap stone) are the major driving resources behind the industries based in the city. As for composition of industries is concerned, then large scale industries make up only 7 to 8 units amongst thousands of industries spread across the district. USD ($US) : 1.3

Sagar

Agriculture forms the backbone of Sagar economy. Many districts completely rely on the income generated from the agriculture taken up in the city. The farmers use latest technologies pertaining to the sector of agriculture so that a healthy crop is obtained. A strong agriculture economy has led to the improvement in the living standards of people living in the city of Sagar. The chief crops grown here are chickpeas, wheat, oilseeds and soghum. Sagar is also into poultry farming, animal husbandry, dairy farming, fisheries, forestry and cattle fairs.With many proposed large and small scale industries, the economy of Sagar is bound to grow at a fast pace. It is also a major hub for useful minerals. Due to its scenic beauty and proximity to Khajuraho tourism also contributes in strengthening its economy. In Madhya Pradesh, Sagar is the sixteenth largest district in size.These small scale industries mainly manufacture steel utensils, detergent cake and powder, agricultural equipments, welding electrodes, plastic goods, alum, caustic soda, solvent plant, granitbillie stone, pipes, acrylic sheets, PVC cable, acrylic products, incense sticks, all purpose flour etc. Bidi (A traditional Tobacco used in India) making is one of the most traditional and eminent business in Sagar and is done almost all over Sagar..... GDP ($US) : 1.1 billion.

MACRO-ECONOMIC TREND

This is a chart of trend of gross state domestic product of Madhya Pradesh at market prices estimated by *Ministry of Statistics and Programme Implementation* with figures in millions of Indian Rupees:

Year	*Gross State Domestic Product*
1980	77,880
1985	139,050
1990	304,720
1995	478,410
2000	737,150

Note 1: Includes Chattisgarh

Madhya Pradesh's gross state domestic product for 2004 is estimated at $32 billion in current prices. After partition, the new Madhya Pradesh state produces about 70% of the output of the old Madhya Pradesh state - the rest is produced by Chattisgarh.

Children in an Opium Field in Malwa: The region is one of the world's major opium producers. It was this crop that resulted in close connections between the economies of Malwa, the western Indian ports and China, bringing international capital to the region in the 18th and 19th centuries. Malwa opium was a challenge to the monopoly of the East India Company, which was supplying Bengal opium to China. This led the British company to impose many restrictions on the production and trade of the drug; eventually, opium trading was pushed underground. When smuggling became rife, the British eased the restrictions.

Today, the region is still one of the largest producers of legal opium in the world. There is a central, government-owned opium and alkaloid factory in the city of Neemuch. Nevertheless, there is a still a significant amount of illicit opium production, which is channelled into the black market. The headquarters of India's Central Bureau of Narcotics is in Mandsaur.

The region is predominantly agricultural. The black, volcanic soil is ideal for the cultivation of cotton, and textile manufacture is an important industry. Large centres of textile production include Indore, Ujjain and Nagda. Maheshwar is known for its fine *Maheshwari* saris, and Mandsaur for its coarse woollen blankets. Handicrafts are an important source of income for the tribal population.

Coloured lacquerware from Ratlam, rag dolls from Indore, and papier-mache articles from Indore, Ujjain and several other centres are well known. The brown soil in parts of the region is particularly suitable for the cultivation of such *unalu* (early summer) crops as wheat, gram (*Cicer arietinum*) and til (*Sesamum indicum*). Relatively poor soil is used for the cultivation of *syalu* such (early winter) crops as millet (*Andropogon sorghum*), maize (*Zea mays*), mung bean (*Vigna radiata*), urad (*Vigna mungo*), batla (*Pisum sativum*) and peanuts (*Arachis hypogaea*). Overall, the main crops are jowar, rice, wheat, coarse millet, peanuts and pulses, soya bean, cotton, linseed, sesame and sugarcane.

Sugar mills are located in numerous small towns. Mandsaur district is the sole producer in India of white- and red-coloured slate, used in the district's 110 slate pencil factories. There is a cement factory in. Apart from this, the region lacks mineral resources. The region's industries mainly produce consumer goods—but there are now many centres of large- and medium-scale industries, including Indore, Nagda, and Ujjain.

Indore has a large-scale factory that produces diesel engines. Pithampur, an industrial town 25 km from Indore, is known as the Detroit of India for its heavy concentration of automotive industry. Indore is recognised as the commercial capital of Madhya Pradesh, and is the main centre for trade in textiles and agro-based products. It has one of the six Indian Institutes of Management.

Value Added Tax in Madhya Pradesh

Madhya Pradesh Value Added Tax Act

VAT Tax payable on value addition.

Value Addition is not profit it is difference between sale prices and purchase price.

Methods of Charging Vat

1. *Subtraction Method :* In this method tax is charged on difference of Sale Price and Purchase Price. *i.e.* Taxable Amount = Net Sales- Net Purchase
2. *Tax Credit Method:* In this method tax on Sales is separately calculated and there from Input tax rebate is subtracted.

INPUT TAX REBATE (ITR) [Sec. 14] An input tax rebate is available on local purchase of goods on which tax is being paid. ITR shall be available for full amount of tax paid on a. Purchase of Raw Material. b. Packing Material. c. Incidental goods. d. Consumable stores and Plant and Machinery. e. Goods purchased for use as plant, machinery, equipments and parts thereof.

ITR shall be available even if finished goods are transferred outside the state (SOS). But, in that case ITR shall be available only in respect of tax paid in excess of 4%.

ITR is available on purchase itself and one need not to wait till sale of said goods.

ITR is not available in case of following: a. Goods received as sample. b. Goods received as replacement. c. Goods used for manufacturing or processing of goods given as free sample, gift or replacement. d. Goods procured from out-side the state. e. ITR will not be available if tax is not shown separately in purchase bill/invoice.

ITR in Respect of Plant & Machinery

Plant and machinery, equipments and parts thereof will also be eligible For input tax rebate. The Plant and Machinery, equipments, etc. Shall be eligible for rebate in same quarter in which it is Purchased irrespective of when they are put to use. ITR will be available to the extent of tax paid in excess of 4%, if a. Finished goods are tax-free. b. Packing material used to pack tax-free goods. c. Machinery is used for Production of tax-free goods. ITR in case of manufacture of goods for other on job basis will be available because there is no condition for sale by dealer.

How and When to Claim ITR

A dealer who is liable to pay tax quarterly can claim ITR and adjust it against tax payable by him.

In case of dealer who is liable to pay monthly tax, the amount of ITR should be calculated for each month and should be adjusted against tax payable for that month.

If ITR is not claim within that month or quarter it can be claimed in next month or quarter.

How to Calculate ITR

ITR need not be calculated on one to one basis it will be calculated on the total sales and total purchase basis. Sales value is of importance in this case.

Carry Forward/refund of ITR

Except in case of export of goods or pertaining to plant & machinery, refund of ITR shall not be allowed in same year.

Amount of ITR shall be adjusted under CST or VAT but not against entry tax. Unadjusted ITR can be carried forward till two years and then it can be refunded.

Payment of Tax

Tax is payable in challan in Form 26. Tax is payable monthly if tax amount 15000/- or more. In default payment of tax interest is charged @ 1.5% per month of the tax payable from day tax is due.

ITR in Respect of Opening Stock

ITR in respect of Opening Stock is available on date of commencement of the VAT act. ITR on Opening Stock will be available for: 1. Registered Dealers 2. In respect of goods of nature tax paid goods in MPCT Act. 3. Goods purchased after 1/4/05. 4. Goods are for resale 5. Opening Stock should not include Capital Goods. 6. Opening stock including raw/packing material, finished goods, WIP (as finished goods).

Calculation of ITR on Finished Goods & WIP

ITR in respect of Finished Goods shall be calculated as following:

> *First of all the quantity of raw material and packing material used for manufacturing have to determined and amount of input material from registered dealers in M.P. by paying tax will have to be determined, and then their purchase price will have to be determined on any suitable basis, like FIFO and tax paid thereon have to be calculated.*

ITR on Opening Stock How and When to be availed.

ITR in respect of opening stock is to be availed in 3 equal installments within the 9 months from date of commencement of the act. If such rebate cannot be availed in year 2006-07 then it can be carried forward to next year. ITR in respect of Opening Stock shall be availed in Form 66 by 30th May. If tax is not shown separately in the bills. As per Rule 82(6) if tax is not shown separately in purchase bill pertaining to opening.

Narmada Dam Project

The Narmada Dam Project, is a project involving the construction of a series of large hydroelectric dams on the Narmada River (Narbada River) in India.

Sardar Sarovar Project (SSP) is the largest multipurpose project involved in the construction. The project was first conceived of in the 1940s by the country's first prime minister, Jawaharlal Nehru.

The project only took form in 1979 as part of a development scheme to increase irrigation and produce hydroelectricity. Of the 30 large dams planned on river Narmada, Sardar Sarovar is the largest. With a proposed height of 136.5 m, it's also high on discord between the planners and the Narmada Bachao Andolan. The multi-purpose project will irrigate more than 18,000 square kilometres - most of it in drought prone areas like - Kutch and Saurashtra.

Benefits of the Dam

The expected benefits of the dam as listed in the Judgement of Supreme Court of India are as follows: " The benefits expected to flow from the implementation of the Sardar Sarovar Project had been estimated as follows:

- *Irrigation:* 1,792,000 km^2 of land spread over 12 districts, 62 talukas and 3393 villages (75% of which is drought-prone areas) in Gujarat and 730 km^2 in the arid areas of Barmer and Jalore districts of Rajasthan.

Characteristics

Drinking water facilities to 8215 villages and 135 urban centres in Gujarat both within and outside command. These include 5825 villages and 100 urban centres of Saurashtra and

Kachchh which are outside the command. In addition, 881 villages affected due to high contents of fluoride will get potable water.

- Power Generation: 1450 megawatts.
- Annual Employment
  - o 600,000 man-years in post construction.
- Protection against advancement of little Rann of Kutch and Rajasthan desert.
- Flood protection to riverine reaches measuring 300 km^2, 210 villages including Bharuch city and 750,000 population.
- Benefits to:
  a) Dhumkhal Sloth Bear Sanctuary.
  b) Wild Ass Sanctuary in Little Rann of Kachchh
  c) Black Buck Sanctuary at Velavadar.
  d) Great Indian Bustard Sanctuary in Kachchh
  e) Nal Sarovar Bird Sanctuary.
- Development of fisheries: Deepening of all village tanks of command which will increase their capacities, conserve water, will recharge ground water, save acquisition of costly lands for getting earth required for constructing canal banks and will reduce health hazard.
- Facilities of sophisticated communication system in the entire command.
- Increase in additional annual production on account of (the dam)
  - o Agricultural production- Rupees 9,000,000,000, Domestic water supply-Rupees 1,000,000,000, Power Generation -Rupees 4,400,000,000 thus totalling Rupees 14,000,000,000."

Height of Concern

- In February 1999, the Supreme Court of India gave the go ahead for the dam's height to be raised to 88 metres from the initial 80.

- In October 2000 again, in a 2 to 1 majority judgement in the Supreme Court, the government was allowed to construct the dam up to 90 metres.
- In May 2002, the Narmada Control Authority approved increasing the height of the dam by another five metres.
- In March 2004, the Authority allowed another raise - this time to 110 metres.
- In March 2006, the Narmada Control Authority gave clearance for the height of the dam to increased from 110.64 metres to 121.92. (This comes after the Supreme Court of India had refused to stay the height of the Dam again in 2003)
- In September 2006, the people living alongside the river were experiencing very high rise floods. The Narmada Control Authority believe that below the dam a leak of some hundreds of litres of water got through.

Criticism of the Dam

The Narmada dam is India's most controversial dam project and its environmental impact and net costs and benefits are widely debated. The Narmada Dam has been the centre of controversy and protest since the late 1980s.

Local protests taking the form of a movement, known as the *Narmada Bachao Andolan* (Save Narmada Movement) have been led by Medha Patkar. The World Bank was a funder of the SSP, but withdrew after an independent review in 1990. Indian writer Arundhati Roy has protested the Narmada Dam project.

Spanner Films's documentary Drowned Out (2002) follows one tribal family who decide to stay at home and drown rather than make way for the Narmada Dam.

Author Arundhati Roy wrote a protest of the Narmada Dam Project in her book *The Cost of Living* (Modern Library, 1999).

The Supreme Court gave clearance for the height to be increased to 121.92mts, but in the same judgment, Mr. Justice

Bharucha has given directions that the Grievance Redressal Authorities of Gujarat, Madhya Pradesh and Maharashtra should, after inspection, certify, before further construction of the dam begins, that all those ousted by the huge increase in height by 5mts from the present level have already been satisfactorily rehabilitated, and also that suitable vacant land for rehabilitating all those who will be ousted by the increase in the height by another 5 meters is already in the possession of the respective States.

This process shall be repeated for every successive 5-metre increase in height. This observation has nothing new to offer, in substance; As "The Narmada Water Disputes Tribunal Award" states that land should be made available to the oustees at least a year in advance before submergence (Clause XI, Subclause IV(2) (iv), Subclause IV(6)(i), (ii)).

Of equal concern is the rehabilitation process that has been carried out. The SC guidelines state that "every displaced family whose more than 25% of agricultural land holding was acquired would be entitled to be allotted irrigable land of its choice to the extent of the land acquired subject to the prescribed ceiling with a minimum of two hectares land and that PAFs' would be allotted a house/plot free of cost".

Now the report (courtesy, The Hindu. Full text at) submitted by the Group of Ministers (GoM), that visited the resettlement and rehabilitation (R&R) sites in Madhya Pradesh, has some of the following observations:

"The GoM visited Khalghat site where Madhya Pradesh Government had offered land to 407 families. Only 2 families had accepted the land. The top soil there is black. The people say that they have to dig 10 feet deep to find the cultivable land"

"It was for the first time that the GoM heard from Shri Mohan Lal that the Income Tax Department deducted Rupees One lakh from every unit of 10 lakhs that was paid to the oustees by way of compensation and for purchase of land. It was Shri Mohan Lal again who said that people were pressurized to accept cash. He said that a bribe of Rs.20,000/- had to be paid for receipt of every cheque that was given to the oustees"

"the GoM went to Dharampuri. It is the largest area selected by the Madhya Pradesh Government for settlement of oustees and 4,000 PAFs are slated to be settled there (No, they are shown to have been settled there already). Not a single plot of land has been occupied by any PAF"

The Madhya Pradesh Chief Minister has said that the GoM formed its opinion of the R&R process based on visits to limited number of sites but still, the fact remains that there are at least these many families left to be rehabilitated.

Further raising of the height of the Narmada Dam, as permitted would also result in the forest area of Hoshangabad being completely destroyed.

OTHER AGRICULTURAL INPUTS

Implements

Pesticides: The Corporation has so far established 5 Agro based units with its own resources and 4 units in the Joint sector.

The Corporation is now focusing more on the promotion of Agro industrial units in the Joint and Assisted Sectors. For this purpose, the Corporation solicits proposals from:

Prospective Investors

Export Oriented Fruits and Vegetables Processing Units

Integrated Horticultural Farms

Mushroom Production and Processing

Tissue Culture

Units Based on Existing Agri-Products Like Tamarind, Mango, Minor Forest Produce.

The Corporation owns a mechanised farm of 3300 acres at Babai, district Hoshangabad about 100 KMs from Bhopal. The farm is fully irrigated and is especially suitable for Horticultural

Crops. Proposals from "any person " were invited for taking up integrated activities on this farm will be considered.

Only one *S&P CNX 500* conglomerate has its corporate office in Madhya Pradesh *viz.* Ruchi Soya Industries (2005 gross income Rs.49,661 million).

Minor Forest Produce

MFP from the forests, such as Tendu leaves used to roll bidi's, Sal seed, teak seed and lak are a major contributor to the rural economy of the state.

INFRASTRUCTURE

Energy

Power generation in MP (31 March 2018)

Power	Capacity (MW)
Thermal	12,805.41
Renewable	4,019.80
Hydro	3,223.66
Nuclear	273.0

The state has a total installed power generation capacity of 20321.87 MW as of 31 March 2018. The Madhya Pradesh Electric Board is located at Jabalpur.

TRANSPORT

Road network of Madhya Pradesh

Road type	Length (in km)
National Highways	5,027
State Highways	10,429
Major District Roads	19,241

Bus and train services cover most of Madhya Pradesh. The 99,043-kilometre-long (61,542 mi) road network of the state includes 20 national highways. A 4,948-kilometre-long (3,075 mi) rail network criss-crosses the state, with Jabalpur serving as headquarters for the West Central Railway Zone of the Indian Railways. The Central Railway and the Western Railway also cover parts of the state. Most of the western Madhya Pradesh comes under Ratlam Rail Division of Western Railways, including cities like Indore, Ujjain, Mandsaur, Khandwa, Neemuch and Bairagarh in Bhopal. The state has a total of 20 major railway junctions. The major inter-state bus terminals are located in Bhopal, Indore, Gwalior and Jabalpur. More than 2000 buses are conducted daily from these four cities. The intra-city transit systems mostly consist of buses, private autos and taxis.

The state does not have a coastline. Most of the sea trade happens through the Kandla and Jawaharlal Nehru Port (Nhava Sheva) in the neighbouring states, which are well-connected to MP by road and rail networks.

Madhya Pradesh being sourounded by land has both Land and Air transport facility. Buses and Trains are well spread all over the MP. Air Transport is at Indore, Bhopal, Jabalpur, Gwalior and Khajuraoo.

Demographics: The majority of the population of Madhya Pradesh are Hindus. Hindus contribute nearly 90 percent of the state population. Muslims are nearly 6 percent and rest are Sikhs, Jains, Zoroastrians, Christians and Buddhists.

Languages: The predominant language of the region is Hindi. In addition to standard Hindi, several regional variants are spoken, which are considered by some to be dialects of Hindi, and by others to be distinct but related languages. Among these languages are Malvi in Malwa, Nimadi in Nimar, Bundeli in Bundelkhand, and Bagheli and Avadhi in Bagelkhand and the southeast. Each of these languages or dialects has dialects of its own. Other languages include Bhilodi (Bhili), Gondi, and the isolate Kalto (Nahali), all spoken by tribal groups. Due to rule of Marathas, Marathi is spoken by a substantial number of people.

Aviation

The Devi Ahilyabai Holkar Airport at Indore is the busiest airport in Madhya Pradesh. Raja Bhoj International Airport in

Bhopal, Dumna Airport in Jabalpur, Gwalior Airport and Khajuraho Airport also have scheduled commercial passenger services. Besides these, minor airstrips are located at Sagar, Ratlam, Mandsaur, Ujjain, Khandwa, Rewa, Shivpuri and Satna.

Other

The state has 51 district hospitals, 333 community health centres, 1,155 primary health centres and 8,860 sub-centres.

The urban infrastructure has improved considerably in the past decade. 22 projects costing above $500 million have been sanctioned under the Jawaharlal Nehru National Urban Renewal Mission for the development of Bhopal, Indore, Jabalpur and Ujjain.

Seven Cities of Madhya Pradesh Bhopal, Indore, Gwalior, Jabalpur, Satna, Ujjain, and Sagar have been selected under Smart cities mission

Media

Dainik Bhaskar, Dainik Jagran, Nava Bharat, Nai Duniya, Rajasthan Patrika, raj express, are the leading Hindi newspapers. Other local newspapers are published in the cities. In English Times of India, Hindustan Times, The Hitavada, Central Chronicle and *Free Press* have editions from Bhopal with The Hitavada also being in Jabalpur. A Sindhi daily, is published from Bhopal is the only Sindhi newspaper in state.

INFORMATION TECHNOLOGY IN MP AGRO

The Corporation has started its computerization in the year 1994-95 with a single computer in its Corporate Office at Bhopal. With a strong target in mind to achieve more heights in this field, the Corporation has increased the activity in its Corporate Office. The Corporation is pioneer in adopting the most modern information technology in the entire state offices at one time. All the District Offices are equipped with computers, modem & fax facilities.

The Corporation has already established dialup connection between field functionaries and HO with Internet/Email devices for data transmission from centre to Head Office and vice versa. Appropriate software have been provided to District Offices to computerize almost whole area of operation such as Accounting, MIS, DIS, Store Accounting & Reporting to Head Office. It has resulted in a significant improvement in the monitoring system of the organisation.

The Corporation has also established a strong Local Area Network in its Corporate office by computerizing the entire work.

From the year 2000-01 the Corporation has been providing technical know-how to the departments of Agriculture, Horticulture, Excise, Cooperative Society, Rural Road Development and alike of the Government of Madhya Pradesh right from system study to establish and computerize their day-today operation.

INDUSTRY

Forests are important in the state. About 1.7 million hectares of land in the state is under forests. Apart from the high quality teak, 'sal' an important timber wood is also available in the state. Bamboos are also available in large quantities. A product of the forests of great relevance to the economy and even the polities of the state is the tendu leaves used extensively for making beedies. The state's forests are mainly located in the Vindhyas and the Satpuras.

Coal and iron are among the more important of the minerals of Madhya Pradesh. The iron ore found in Madhya Pradesh is of high grade and occurs in the Dury, Jubalpur, Bastar and Gwalior districts. Manganese is another important mineral which occurs in Madhya Pradesh in the Balaghat and Chhindwara districts. There is bauxite which is required in the production of aluminium and which is available in the Katni tehsil of Jabalpur. Madhya Pradesh has a large deposit of limestone required for the production of cement. The Panna region has a rich diamond bed and is well known for the production of diamonds. Marble is also available in the state in several districts. The state has rich granaries of food. In the northern part sillimanite and ochre are excavated. Other natural products are steatite and China clay.

There are many flourishing textile mills in the state and artificial silk manufacturing plants located at Ujjain, Nagda, Indore and Gwalior. In the public sector, huge plants, namely the Bhilai Steel plant, the Heavy Electrical and the Bailadilla are the major achievements. The Nepa Mills produces newsprint for the country. Diesel engines are manufactured at Indore and attractive pottery and carpets are produced at Gwalior.

The state is famous for traditional village crafts such a chanderi sarees, leather and clay toys. Ancillary industries such as dyeing, calico printing and bleaching have also tended to concentrate in areas producing handloom cloth, silk and wool products. The states wood work and lacquer-ware are also very famous.

MP Agro Industry: The Madhya Pradesh State Agro Industries Development Corporation Ltd. is a wholly Government company headquartered at the State Capital Bhopal which is actively engaged in promoting the agro-potential of Madhya Pradesh

Major Activities of M.P. Agro: Marketing of Agricultural inputs such as Seeds, Pesticides, Agricultural Machineries, Tractors, Irrigation systems such as Pumpsets, Sprinkler and Drip system and Chemical and Organic Fertilizers.

Manufacture of High Quality BIO-FERTILIZERS such as Rhizobium, Azatobacter, PSB and Liquid Culture

Manufacture of ORGANIC-MANURE from Farm Waste and City Garbage.

Large scale production of Hybrid Vegetable Seeds, Planting Material for Fruits and Commercial Scale Production of Vegetables and Fruits for the Domestic and International market at India's largest farm (3500 acres).

Promotion of AGRO PROCESSING INDUSTRIES as per the schemes of Ministry of Food Processing Industries, Govt. of India in Madhya Pradesh with special emphasis on units for Pulping, Brining and Freezing of Fruits, Vegetables and Floriculture.

What MP Agro can Offer?

Supply of Cereals, Oilseeds, Pulses, Fruits, Vegetables, Spices and Flowers sourced in Madhya Pradesh to National and International buyers.

Complete services for Project Promotion of Agro based industries.

Equity participation on a High Quality Seed and Horticultural planting material.

Marketing opportunity for High Quality Seed and Horticultural planting material.

Contract farming tie-up with Government farms and Private cultivators for dedicated cultivation of Cereals, Fruits, Flowers and Vegetables.

What MP Agro is looking for:

Long term tie-up with Domestic and International partners to market the Processed Produce of Madhya Pradesh.

Collaboration for developing Hybrids Seeds for fruits and vegetables. Partnership for setting up Tissue Culture Facility for Horticultural Crops.

Investment and Technology for setting up large capacity Processing Plants for handling the Vegetables and Fruit production of the State. Private participation in setting up organic manure plants on urban solid waste of Municipal Corporations.

BIDI INDUSTRY

Bidi Industry occupies the key place among the small scale forest based cottage industries of Madhya Pradesh. The industry, which is basically labour intensive, absorbs the highest proportion of workers in total industrial workforce of the State.

Bidi industry had the highest proportion of Gross Value Added to the Total Value Added as industrial sector as a whole. Madhya Pradesh has a vast forest area along with Tendu leaves area and is known for its vast Tendu leaves production.

The prospects of the Bidi industry in Madhya Pradesh are quite high provided attention is paid to this industry as the close substitute to Bidi are the machine made cigarettes by the large giants like MNCs. The present study aims at finding out the extent of technical change and growth pattern of productivity in the Bidi Industry of Madhya Pradesh with the help of ASI data for the period of 1973-74 to 1992-93.

On the basis of results, it can be concluded that labour is the major source of output growth as compared to capital. The time trend coefficient is either found negative or insignificant in most of the cases and suggests inferences in favour of technological retrogression.

Thus, it can be concluded that there is a need of review the mechanical, managerial and technological aspects with a view to promote R & D efforts in this industry otherwise this industry will also ride on the same track as the industrial sector of country as well as State

Wood Carving: Wood carving is one of the main industry of the tribes of Madhya Pradesh. Various objects of daily use, hut dwellings etc. are finely carved. Tobacco containers with tortoise and the sun-moon motifs and designs, Combs depicted with animal motifs, intensely carved wooden spears and utensils, carved boxes, panels, furniture and funerary pillars carved with figures are some of the products.

Brass Work: Brass work occupies an important place in the craftsmanship of the Bastar tribes. The urge for creativeness reflects in most of the images made of the brass and bell metal. For preparing these figures they follow the ancient cire-perdue process. First the earthen core is made, then wax is shaped on the object which is ultimately replaced by molten metal. The products include, animal and human figures, deities etc.

Textiles: Textile weaving is one of the main crafts of Madhya Pradesh. Sarees in subtle shades are woven in places like Chanderi, a village near Gwalior and Maheshwar. These sarees include a wide variety of checks with traditional gold borders. Madhya Pradesh's craftsmen are equally adept at producing tassar silk handloom fabrics.

Thousands of craftsmen practice hand printing, generally with vegetable dyes. Tarapur and Umedpura, two villages on the opposite banks of the river Gujari, use indigo for their prints. The printers specialise in printing fabrics with a blue background and yellow and red prints, known as nandra. Garments, bedspreads, tablecloths and curtain material are produced here. Jawad also has a similar style of printing. Mandsaur produces excellent bandhanis as well as resist prints imitating the bandhani patterns. Sarees with batik work based on the local mandana traditions of floor and wall decorations have been developed here. Tie and dye chunaries are the speciality of Tarapur and Mandsaur. Skilled craftsmanship is also on display in a variety of zari-embroidered articles.

Carpet Weaving: Carpet weaving has became popular in Gwalior. The fine quality of weaving in imaginative designs has earned Gwalior's carpet industry an excellent reputation. Today, more than a thousand looms are in operation in and around the city.

TRADE AND INDUSTRY

Betul district's economy is predominantly an agrarian one and due to the large forest cover, it is somewhat also based on forests. Betul is well connected by Road & Rail network. It is Delhi-Chennai broadgage railway line & National highway No.69 also passes through this district. The nearest Air-Ports are at Nagapur & Bhopal almost 180 Kms., From the district headquarter betul.

With Abundant Food: Grain production & extensive coverage of forest wended with good Road & Rail Network, better Telecomm facilities in Betul is praised to become an industrial advanced district. Few highlights on Industrial development of the District are as follows:

- There are 7160 cottage industries in the district, which have provided employment to 17,682 people and have a total investment over 1235.65 Lakhs.
- There are 33 Small Scale Industries (SSI) in the district have provided employment to 667 people and have total investment over 819.99 Lakhs. Out of 33 SSI's 8 are Agro based, 13 are Mineral based, 1 is forest based and 11 are others.
- There are 5 Large & Medium scale units in the district have provided employment to 999 people and have total investment over 1681.37 Lakhs. Details of them as follows:

Industroa, Areas

Movement of Industrial Goods: The movement of Industrial Goods produced in this district by enlarge done by Road Transport mode. Few Industries mainly Large & Medium Industries use Rail networks for transporting their finishing products. Exporting units mainly Tyre Industry use water ways, which are exported to USA, UK, MIDDLE EAST, African countries. The shipping of exporting goods is normally done through MUMBAI, CHENNAI & VIZAG see ports.

ORGANIC-MANURE

The M.P. State Agro Industries Development Corporation limited may continue to be empowered to work as a Nodal Agency for sourcing of appropriate technology, selection of entrepreneurs and assisting them in getting all the facilities needed to set up solid waste management project in the town. Eighteen cities and towns inn Madhya Pradesh having a population more than one lakh produce around 219,000 tones of solid waste yearly. The present system of disposal by open dumping, creates a lot of environmental problems and public health hazards. There is necessary to take proper steps to solve this problem. Such a massive programme covering all the towns and cities of MP will need huge investment, private participation.

The Corporation is the pioneer in setting up of Organic Manure plants based on solid waste one at Bhopal and another at Gwalior with the total capacity of processing 220 MT of solid waste per day. Organic manure being produced is sold to the farmers of MP with the help of its district offices as well as with the help of private dealers. The retail price to the end-user is Rs.2800/- per MT while the ex-factory price to the dealers is Rs.1600/- per MT. As Nodal Agency for urban solid waste management, the Corporation is also looking for private parties for running the existing plants and also for promoting new projects in all major districts of Madhya Pradesh in Joint/ Assisted sector.

Bio-fertilizers: The Corporation has set up a Bio-fertilizer Plant at Bhopal in the year 1985-86 with an installed capacity of 800 MT per year. Since inception, it has been continuously winning Best Productivity Award from the National Productivity Council, Government of India. The plant has enough expertise to do research and development on Bio-fertilizer. The main R&D being done are as below:

1. Carrier formulation and enrichment for different types of bio-fertilizers.

2. Research for increase of shelf life of bio-fertilizer.
3. Study of growth pattern of different types of microbial isolates used in commercial production of bio-fertilizers.
4. Isolation and identification of different microbial isolates involved in decomposition of bio-degradable city garbage.
5. Establishment of Tissue culture laboratory for commercially viable horticultural crops. Establishment of bio-technology park for women entrepreneurs in the State of Madhya Pradesh.

Fertilizers: The Corporation is providing chemical and organic fertilizers to the farmers through its field functionaries. The Corporation is mainly providing following fertilizers: UREA D.A.P. M.O.P. SSP. For bio-fertilizers we are the largest producer at National level and have received in continuation 20 awards from National Productivity Council. The Corporation has sold 243115 MTs of various fertilizers in the year 2003-04 and planned to sell 300000 MTs Fertilizers in 2004-05. Corporation is having a wide network of more than 300 outlets for sale of fertilizers and other inputs.

Tractors: The corporation since its inception (1969) has been supplying tractors, initially importer ones and then indigenous tractors.

The corporation has so far supplied more than 28000 tractors in the state of Madhya Pradesh. Under the centrally sponsored Macro Management scheme, tractors upto 35 HP are being supplied, to the farmer on subsidy of Rs. 30,000. Preference is given to the farmers belonging to SC, ST and other weaker section of society under this subsidy schemes, the corporation is supplying tractors approved by the Govt. of India *viz.* Eicher, Swaraj, Mahindra, Tafe, Escorts, HMT, Sonalika, Ford, New Holland, Bajaj Tempo, L&T John Deer, Indo Farm, Same Dentz, Shaktiman (Mahindra Gujarat) & VST.

Besides tractors, under the same schemes the corporation is also supplying various types the corporation is also supplying various types of power tillers, power drawn agricultural implements/equipments to the farmers against subsidy.

Custom-hiring & Servicing: The Corporation is providing well-boring machines yield testing machines/JCB machine Bulldozers, caterpillars, etc. on hire basis to the farmers. For this purpose, the Corporation holding following machines which are available on booking with any of the branch.

Biogas Development Programme: The Government of Madhya Pradesh has appointed as Nodal Agency for the development of biogas programme in the State of Madhya Pradesh.

The Corporation has so far installed 1,72,064 (TILL 2003-04) family type biogas plants against the estimated potential of 14,91,000 plants in the State. In view of the potential exists, the Corporation has made a quantum jump in the installation of biogas plants, *i.e.* about 8600 plants per year

1.1 *Objectives:* Objectives of Biogas Development Programme are follows:

(i) To provide fuel for cooking purpose and organic manure to rural households through biogas plants;

(ii) To mitigate drudgery of rural women, reduce pressure on forest and accentuate social benefits;

(iii) To recycle human waste through linking of toilets with biogas plants for improving sanitation.

1.2 *Potential and Achievement:* A total of 151070 family type biogas plants have been installed in the State against the estimated potential of 14,91,200 biogas plants. Thus the coverage of potential achieved so far is about 10%.

Till the year 85-86, 20133 biogas plants were installed in the State and from the year 85-86 till 97-98, 106767 plants have been installed by this Corporation.

1.3 *Estimated Costs of Family Type Biogas Plants:* The cost of biogas plants varies according to model and retention period, capacity, market prices of construction materials and labour cost. On an average, estimated cost of a common 2 cubic meter capacity family type Fixed Dome Deenbandhu Biogas Plant is about Rs. 8,500/

1.4. Biogas and Manure Management Programme (NBMMP)

a). *Training Courses :* The financial support will be provided by GoI for organizing following training programme.

Training Programme	*Duration*	*Purpose*
Users Training	One Day	To educate the user about the Benefits, Operations & Maintenance of Plant
Construction cum		
Maintenance training	16 Day	to training of untrained mason

b). Incentive for saving diesel by using biogas in dual fuel engines—Incentive will be given for purchase of plastic or rubber balloon, container for storage and transportation of biogas from the site of the plants to the site of the engine subject to a maximum of Rs. 2500/- per plant.

1.4.1. Programme Components:

Central and State subsidy 98-99

Central Subsidy		*Total Subsidy Payable to Beneficiaries*					
S.no	*Capa-city*	*Sc/St*	*Smf/Ll*	*Gen.*	*Sc/St*	*Smf/Ll*	*Gen.*
1	1 CUM	2300	2300	1800	2300	2300	2000
2	2 CUM	2300	2300	1800	3000	3000	2200
3	3 CUM	2300	2300	1800	3300	2300	2400
4	4 TO 10CUM	2300	2300	1800	3300	2300	2400

(ii) Cattle Dung Based Biogas Plants Linked With Toilets

An additional subsidy of Rs. 500/- is provided for cattle dung based biogas plants linked with sanitary toilets.

1.5. *Programme For 2004-05:* Target of 12,000 biogas plants has been fixed by MNES for this State.

Activity Of Bullock-drawn, Improved Agricultural Implements And Hand Tools.

This Corporation is playing an important role in promoting the crop production programme taken-up by small & marginal farmers by providing them improved Agricultural implement so as to enable to save their time, energy and money. In order to achieve farm operations timely & effectively, scientifically improved implements suitable for various crop zones finalized by

Directorate of Agril. Engg. and C.I.A.E. are being supplied by the corporation to the needy farmers.

Under various centrally sponsored subsidy schemes of Govt. of India and Regional Scheme of State Govt. following bullock drawn improved implements and hand tools are made available to majority of farmers on subsidy worth Rs.150.00 or 25% cost of implements subject to max. limit Rs.1500=00).

Name of agricultural implements meant for various agricultural operation *i.e.* land preparation, seed sowing, water supply, inter culture, etc. which are being sold on subsidy are illustrated below:-

S.No.	*Name of implements*	*S.No.*	*Name of implements*
1.	M.P. Plough	10.	M.B. Plough
2.	Improved Hal	11.	Dora
3.	Improved Bakher	12.	Hand wheel Hoe
4.	Bund Farmers	13.	Soya Weeder
5.	Low Lift Water Pump	14.	Hand Hoe
6.	Automatic seed-cum-fert. Drill	15.	Maize Sheller
7.	Dufan	16.	Ground nut Digger
8.	Tifan	17.	Ground nut Decorticator
9.	Narihals	18.	Paddy Puddler

Most of the BD Implements and hand tools shown above are being fabricated by the Corporation in its 6 fabrication units located in Bhopal, Indore, Ujjain, Sagar, Chhindwara and Gwalior.

In addition to the above, this Corporation have also been providing following other improved implements to the farmers. There is no subsidy available on these improved implements.

1. Sickle for harvesting crops;
2. Winnowing fan for cleaning grains;
3. Chaff cutter for cutting fodder crops.

Grants Available From Ministry Of Food Processing Industries, Government Of India

(Cases To Be Forwarded Through Mp Agro)

1. Scheme for Technology Upgradation/ Establishment/ Modernization of Food Processing Industries (applicable to all)

The assistance in the form of grant subject to 25% of the cost of plant & machinery, and technical civil work subject to maximum of Rs.50 lacs.

2. Scheme for Human Resource Development

(a) Setting up of Food Processing & Training Centre (FPTC) applicable to Central/State organization, Education & Training Organization, Cooperatives, NGO's

(i) for single product line centre

Grant of Rs. 2.00 lacs for fixed capital costs & Rs. 1.00 lac as revolving seed capital

(ii) for multi product line centre

Grant of Rs.7.50 lacs for fixed capital costs & Rs. 2.00 lacs as revolving seed capital.

3. Scheme for Quality assurance, Codex standards and Research & Development.

(a) Total Quality Management (TQM) : 50% of the total cost towards implementing TQM including ISO-9000, ISO14000, Hazard Analysis and Critical Control Points (HACCP), Good Manufacturing Practices (GMP), Good Hygienic Practices (GHP) with ceiling of Rs.10.00 lacs for Government Organization and 33% with ceiling of Rs.10.00 lacs for other Implementing Agencies.

(b) Promotion of Quality Assurance/Safety Concept. 50% of the cost of project limited to Rs. 3.00 lacs for Government Organizations and 33% limited to Rs.3.00 lacs for Other Agencies.

(c) Bar Coding : 50% of Registration fees and 50% cost of Capital Equipments with a ceiling of Rs. 3.00 lacs for Government Organizations and 50% of the

Registration fees and 33% of cost of Capital Equipments with a ceiling of Rs. 3.00 lacs for all other agencies.

(d) Setting up of Quality Control Laboratory : Assistance limited to entire cost of capital equipments for Government Organizations and 33% of cost of capital equipments for all other agencies.

(e) Research and Development in Processed Food sector: Assistance towards 100% of the capital cost to government organizations, 33% of the capital cost to other implementing agencies.

4. Scheme for Backward and Forward Integration and other Promotional Activities

(a) *Backward Linkage:* Incentive in the form of reimbursement upto 10% of total purchases made by processing unit in a given year, limited to Rs.10.00 lacs for a maximum period of 3 years.

(b) *Forward Integration:* 50% of the cost of the campaign towards market survey, test marketing and brand promotion, subject to a maximum of Rs.50 lacs available to Industry Associations and Representative Bodies.

(c) *Food Fortification:* 50% of the cost of the capital equipment (dosing machine etc.) and its installation charges up to Rs.3.00 lacs available to existing industries engaged in production of cereal/ cereal based products.

5. Scheme for Infrastructure Development:

(a) *Food Park (applicable to all):* 25% of the project cost subject to a maximum of Rs.4.00 crore for provision of common facilities like cold storage, food testing and analysis laboratory, effluent treatment plant, common processing facilities, power, water supply etc. to be set up in Food Parks having minimum area of 30 acres and minimum 20 Food Processing units.

(b) *Packaging Centre (applicable to all):* 25% of the total cost of Plant and Machinery and technical civil works subject to a maximum of Rs. 2 crore for establishing packaging centre, independently and in food parks.

(c) *Modernized Abattoirs:* 25% of the cost of plant and machinery and technical civil works, subject to a maximum of Rs.4 crore for modernizing the existing abattoirs, applicable to local bodies.

(d) *Integrated Cold Chain Facilities:* Ministry's assistance is limited to cold storages for non-horticulture produce or being integral part of the processing unit or special type of cold storages with controlled atmosphere / modified atmosphere facility, grant amounting 25% of the cost of plant and machinery and technical civil works subject to a maximum of Rs.75 lacs, applicable to all agencies.

(e) Value Added Centre

These centres will:

(a) Make value addition leading to enhanced shelf life and higher total realization

(b) Integrate value chain ensuring value addition at each level of handling

(c) Result in information flow and documentation about varieties/ grades, volume traded, method of packaging etc.

(d) facilitate traceability 25% of the cost of plant & machinery and technical civil works subject to a maximum of Rs.50 lacs, applicable to all agencies.

(f) *Irradiation Facilities:* The technology to be guaranteed and its application to be specifically monitored by the Deptt. of Atomic Energy so as to ensure complete safety in the manner of irradiation and the final product. 25% of the cost of plant and machinery and technical civil works for setting up of Irradiation Facilities subject to a maximum of Rs. 5 crores.

Procedure for Submitting Proposals: The MP State Agro Industries Development Corporation Limited, Bhopal is the State

Nodal Agency of Ministry of Food Processing Industries, Government of India, in Madhya Pradesh. Entrepreneur is required to submit application in prescribed format for each one of above mentioned schemes duly supported with all the required documents.

PROGRAMMES/SCHEMES OF NATIONAL HORTICULTURE BOARD

1) Development of Commercial Horticulture through Production and Post Harvest Management.

The scheme will cover high density plantation, micro propagation (tissue culture), hi-tech cultivation under controlled climatic conditions, production through efficient water management techniques, nursery management for quality seed/ plant, hybrid seed production, organic farming, hydroponics for year round quality production, use of plastic in horticulture, bio-technology, genetically modified organisms (GMOs), besides project based on scientific advancement and other projects related to development of infrastructure for production, Post Harvest Management, development of market and primary processing, development of horticulture ancillary industry for improved packaging, corrugated boxes, horticulture machinery, tools etc.

Assistance in the form of back-ended capital investment subsidy not exceeding 20% of the total project cost with a ceiling of Rs.25 lacs per project. Subsidy would be available through participating banks/ FIs in general and through NCDC in case of cooperative sector.

2) Scheme of capital investment subsidy for construction/ extension/ modernization of cold storages/ storages of horticulture produce.

Assistance in the form of 25% back ended capital investment subsidy limited to Rs.50 lacs through banks/FIs in general and through NCDC in case of cooperative sector.

3) Scheme of Technology Development and Transfer for promotion of Horticulture.

Assistance in the form of 100% grant is available as under:

i) Pilot project based on high quality commercial production, for popularizing new and modern scientific concepts in horticulture limited to Rs.10 lacs.

ii) PHM, primary processing, bio-technology and introduction of new tool, equipment, machinery is to be considered on merit

Assistance in the form of 100% grant limited to Rs.25 lacs available to agriculture/horticulture universities, research organizations, agriculture/horticulture departments, PSUs.

iii) R & D projects on specific problems concerning projects based on indigenous fruits, vegetable, flower, medicinal and aromatic plants.

Assistance in the form of 100% grant limited to Rs.25 lacs available to agriculture/horticulture universities, research organizations, agriculture/horticulture departments, PSUs.

Assistance also available for arranging visit of progressive farmers, international visits, experts services from India/ abroad, technology awareness, organizing seminars/ workshops/exhibitions, Udhyan Pandit Competition, publicity, observation cum study tour abroad and for making payment of honorarium to scientists for transferring effective technology on case to case basis.

4. Scheme of establishment of nutritional gardens in rural areas:

Assistance in the form of 100% grant in aid available for supply of fruits plants, vegetable, seeds with ceiling rate of Rs.250 per family, installation of zero energy food chamber for demonstration by panchayat at a total cost of Rs.2500 for 100kg capacity for each unit, demonstrating concept of nutritional gardens with grant limited to Rs.5000/ - through Horti. Deptt / Implementing agencies.

5. Scheme of market information service for horticulture crops.

   NHB through its 33 market information centres is implementing this scheme and making available informations through CD-ROM, monthly/ weekly/ daily bulletin and through internets and websites. Information pertaining to all the important fruits and vegetable are provided.

6. Horticulture promotion services for conducting reviews/ studies concerning horticulture.

   Assistance in the form of 100% grant is available to state government /UTs, central government organizations. NHB empannels consultants for awarding studies as per requirement.

Improving Crop Productivity Through Bee Keeping.

Development of Beekeeping—A Proven Technique to Improve Crop Productivity: About 85% crop plants are cross pollinated as they need to receive pollen from other plants of the same species with the help of external agents. One of the most important such external agent is the honey bees. When the crop is in flowering stage, these pollinators help in early setting of seeds resulting in early and more uniform crop yield. Scientific studies has established 12 crops of economic importance for such as almond, apple, coconut, grape, guava, mango, papaya, mustard, sunflower, cotton, etc. which are specifically benefited from honey bee pollination. The increase in yield of various crops due to pollination by honey bees ranges from 20% to 10%.

M.P. State Agro Ind. Devep Corpn Ltd has been designated as Nodal Agency in the year 2000-01. Initially programme has been implemented with financial assistance from "Agriculture Research and Infrastructure Development Funds" Provided by M.P. State Agriculture Marketing Board. Further M.P. Govt, Department of Agriculture (Horticulture & Form Forestry) has provided necessary funds. The corporation has trained 611 farmers for beekeeping & distributed 663 bee hives with superior quality of "Apis mellifera" bee colonies.

Govt Assistance on Beehives and Bee Colonies: The superior bee colonies (Apis mellifera) produced by selected bee breeders is being distributed to small/ marginal / S.C. / S.T./ Women/ farmers / beekeepers. To encourage purchase of superior bee colonies, subsidy support is being provided at the rate of 25% of the cost subject to maximum Rs. 2.50 & to encourage purchase of standard bee hives with related beekeeping equipment subsidy support at the rate of 25% of the subject to Rs. 350.

Training Courses: The following training courses are scheduled to be conducted for "Development of beekeeping for improving crop productivity" programme:

The above trainings are provided free of cost. The boarding & lodging arrangements are being provided by SDA. For detailed information please write to us or contact our district offices in all districts except Ashoknagar.

Agri Export Zone: The concept of Agri Export Zone attempts to take a comprehensive look at a particular produce/ product located in a contiguous area for the purpose of developing and sourcing the raw material, its processing/packaging, leading to final exports.

However, the entire effort begins with market analyses to assess the market potential for that produce. Subsequently, steps are taken to ascertain the quality parameters that are required for making this produce/product acceptable in the international market.

7

Tourism

TOURISM IN MADHYA PRADESH

The Sanchi stupa

Tourism in Madhya Pradesh has been an attraction of India because of its location in the centre of the country. It has been home to the cultural heritage of Hinduism, Buddhism, Jainism etc. Innumerable monuments, but exquisitely carved temples, stupas, forts & palaces are dotted all over the state. Madhya

Pradesh has won Best Tourism State National award for 3 consecutive years i.e. 2017, 2016 and 2015.

Natural environment

The natural environment of Madhya Pradesh is varied. Consisting largely of a plateau streaked with the mountain ranges of the Vindhyas and the Satpuras, the hills give rise to the main river system - Narmada and the Tapti, running from east to west, and the Chambal, Sone, Betwa, Mahanadi west to east.

One half of the state is forested and offers a unique panorama of wildlife. In the National Parks of Kanha, Bandhavgarh, Shivpuri and many others visitors have the opportunity to see the tiger, the bison and a wide variety of deer and antelope in natural surroundings.

World heritage sites

Kandariya Mahadeva Temple, largest temple in Khajuraho

Although the modern state of Madhya Pradesh came into being in 1956, its cultural heritage is ancient and chequered.

Innumerable monuments, exquisitely carved temples, stupas, forts and palaces on hilltops, raise in the visitors mind visions of empires and kingdoms, of the great warriors and builders, poets and musicians, saints and philosophers; of Hinduism, Buddhism, and Jainism. The famous Sanskrit poet-dramatist Kalidasa and the great musician of the Mughal court, Tansen, were from Madhya Pradesh. They are known all over the world.

Three sites in Madhya Pradesh have been declared World Heritage Sites by UNESCO:

- The Khajuraho Group of Monuments (1986)
- Buddhist Monuments at Sanchi (1989)
- The Rock Shelters of Bhimbetka (2003)

Significant sites

Other architecturally significant or scenic sites include:

- Alampur
- Amarkantak
- Asirgarh
- Bawangaja
- Bhopal
- Chanderi
- Chitrakuta
- Deorkothar
- Dhar
- Gwalior
- Indore
- Jabalpur
- Maheshwar
- Mandleshwar
- Mandu
- Morena
- Muktagiri

- Omkareshwar
- Orchha
- Shivpuri
- Sonagiri
- Ujjain

Madhya Pradesh being very large geographically, and the history being spread over several millennia, a developing a comprehensive picture of heritage and architecture is a monumental task.

National Parks

Madhya Pradesh is home to several National Parks, including:

- Bandhavgarh National Park
- Kanha National Park
- Satpura National Park
- Sanjay National Park
- Madhav National Park
- Van Vihar National Park
- Mandla Plant Fossils National Park
- Panna National Park
- Pench National Park, Madhya Pradesh.
- National Chambal Sanctuary

There are 10 national parks and 25 wildlife sanctuaries in Madhya Pradesh. Apart from tiger, the national parks in Madhya Pradesh have animals like Leopard, Gaur, Chital, Sambar, Nilgai, Chinkara, Barking Deer, Barasingha, Samber Deer, Wild Boar, Monkey, Peacock, etc.

Nature reserves

There are also a number of nature preserves, including:

- Pachmarhi
- Amarkantak
- Bagh Caves

- Bhedaghat
- Bori Wildlife Sanctuary
- Kuno-Palpur Wildlife Sanctuary
- Narwar
- Chambal
- Narsinghgarh

Fairs and festivals

Customs and beliefs in each area in Madhya Pradesh have added colours to the fairs and festivals. Shivratri in Khajuraho, Bhojpur, Pachmarhi and Ujjain; Dusshera in Jabalpur, Ramanavami in Chitrakoot and Orchha, Bhagoriya dance in Jhabua and the annual festival of dances at Khajuraho are events for the tourists to remember. The Malwa festival in Indore, Mandu and Ujjain, and the Pachmarhi festival bring alive the rich folk and tribal culture of the state in colourful celebrations. Gwalior trade fair is India's second largest trade fair. It is organised in various sectors which includes electronic sector, automobile sector, food sector, fun (jhula) sector etc. Gwalior carnival is a newly introduced festival in 2012. It was organised for 22 days in December. It is planned to organise carnival every year. Nimar Utsav takes place every year in the holy city of Maheshwar in the Hindu month of Kartika on the occasion of Kartika Purnima. The festival lasts for 3 days with a cultural programme at Ahilya Ghat in Maheshwar.

EXTERNALLY AIDED PROJECTS

Completed Projects

MP Forestry Project : The World Bank aided MP Forestry project (1995-2000) had a strong component of biodiversity conservation. Under this component, 24 priority Protected Areas were selected for improving their management through scientific management plans, habitat improvement, staff training, provision of enhanced protection infrastructure, and research and monitoring. At present, there are 718 Eco-development

Committees functioning in villages in and around Protected Areas.

India Eco-development Project: The Global Environment Facility (Trust) and the World Bank fund India Eco-development Project. This project has been initiated in 7 selected Project Tiger areas in the country. Pench Project Tiger area in Seoni district of M.P. is one of them. Improved PA management and Eco-development in 99 villages within the buffer zone of the Tiger reserve are two major objectives. The total outlay of this five year project is Rs. 25.45 crores. The Central Government provided funds to the State Government under the 100% Centrally Sponsored Scheme- Eco-development around Protected Areas. The project was launched in 1996 and culminated in June 2004.

Project under Preparation Phase

Biodiversity Conservation and Rural Livelihood Improvement Project: The Government of India has launched a project with a Credit from International Development Association (IDA) and a Grant from the Global Environment Facility (GEF). The project named – "Biodiversity Conservation and Rural Livelihood Improvement Project" will be implemented in 6 selected landscapes of the Country. One of the selected landscapes is the – Satpura Landscape, which includes Satpura Tiger Reserve and parts of adjoining territorial forest division of Hoshangabad, west Chhindwara, and north Betul (Rampur Bhatodi forest managed by M.P. Forest Corporation) in Madhya Pradesh. The total project area will be 2974.50 sq. kms.

In December 2005, Government of India has appointed a consultant to prepare a project document for this project. The project document is under preparation.

Initiatives

Asiatic Lion Reintroduction Project at Kuno-Palpur Sanctuary of Madhya Pradesh: The last of the Asiatic lions are now confined in a small sized protected area, the Gir National Park in Gujarat. The concern towards rapid decline in Asiatic lion population, largely attributed to the fragmentation and destruction of its original extensive range of distribution through out the Indian peninsula, led to a search of a second home for lions. The Wildlife Institute of India, Dehradun carried out a survey in 1993-94 and finally recommended the Kuno - Palpur Sanctuary and its adjoining forests in Sheopur district as the best suited second home for lions. It would be interesting to note that the last lion in Central India was shot in a forest belt near Kuno in 1873.

A lion reintroduction project is now on in the Kuno-Palpur sanctuary totally supported by funds from the Central Government. The Project is for Twenty years.

The work started in 1996-97. The Government of India is funding this project under three existing Centrally Sponsored Schemes- Development of National Parks and Sanctuaries, Ecodevelopment around Protected Areas and the Beneficiary Oriented Scheme for Tribal Development. All 24 villages have been resettled at the relocation site. Relocation work is under progress. The total number of families to be covered under the relocation plan is 1545.

Management actions for minimizing biotic pressures, restoration of habitat, water conservation, enhancement of prey-base and strict protection have already been initiated. The Wildlife Institute of India, Dehradun has conducted the prey-base assessment in January-February, 2005. The site is ready to receive the lions. The Government of Madhya Pradesh has urged the Central Government to expedite transfer of a pride of lions from Gujarat at the earliest.

Establishment of Development Fund: Government of Madhya Pradesh passed an order in 1997 enabling all National Parks and Sanctuaries to directly utilize the receipts from wildlife tourism for development of the Protected Areas. Now, each PA has its own development fund, which can be used for such development works for which funds are not readily available under the normal budget, after getting necessary approval for incurring designated expenditure from a State Level Committee;

Establishment of a Wildlife Health Monitoring, Disease Diagnostic and Research Cell, Jabalpur: To make a beginning towards creating a wild animal health care facility, the MP Forest department has established a Wildlife Health Monitoring, Disease Diagnostic and Research Cell at Veterinary College Jabalpur in collaboration with the JNU Agriculture University. Equipments worth Rs. 62 lakhs have been provided to this cell under the MP Forestry Project. The objectives of the Cell are as follows:

- To evolve a state-wide scenario of diseases of wildlife, particularly of highly endangered Sp. like tiger and hard-ground barasingha.
- To provide technical training to protected area staff in various aspects of wildlife health monitoring and management chemical restraint, autopsy, collection and presentation of body parts of dead animals for lab analysis etc.
- To provide disease diagnostic facilities and services during emergency to PAs, including identification of dead animals from body parts seized in poaching cases.
- To create a database on various parameters related to wild animal health that will help in assessing the health status of wild animals based on hematological and biochemical studies.
- To study the inter-relationship of wild and domestic animal diseases to evolve strategy for prophylactic measures and control methods.
- To evolve a treatment plan for diseases of endangered wild animals in ex-situ conservation areas.
- To develop wildlife forensic facilities

Conservation of Biodiversity in Forests outside the PA Network: The biodiversity conservation concerns of the state cannot be fully satisfied through managing the PAs only that cover about 11.40 percent of the total forest area. The remaining 89% of the forest area is rich repository of biodiversity and therefore biodiversity conservation concerns must be included in the management of territorial forest areas. This led to addition of a chapter on inclusion of biodiversity conservation principles in the management of forests, to the book of guidelines for Working Plan Preparation. In 2006 the WII, Dehradun has published latest guidelines for preparation of wildlife management plans in managed forest areas; this book has been sent to all the field units.

Establishment of Tiger Cell: Increased incidence of poaching of wild animals, especially of highly endangered species like tiger, all over the country is attributed mainly to the high value fetched by the skin, bones and other body parts of these animals in the international market.

International gangs of poacher including the drug mafia are involved in the illicit trade in endangered wildlife.

As M.P. has 19% of India's and 10% of world's tiger population as well as other vulnerable fauna and flora, the state has the accentuated responsibility to provide the best protection to tigers. In order to carry out this responsibility the Police and the Forest departments jointly constituted a "Tiger Cell" in 1994. The major objectives of this Cell are:

- to curb illicit trade in endangered species with special emphasis on tiger.
- networking with national and international agencies involved in eradication of such illicit trade.
- prepare a database of wildlife related crimes as well as criminals and using it for apprehending and prosecuting offenders
- interact and co-ordinate with the authorities in the abutting states in order to evolve and follow a common strategy and also to seek their help in intelligence gathering and arrest of fugitive offenders.

The joint efforts of the police and forest personnel have yielded positive results. The Tiger Cell meets regularly to take account of the progress as well as the shortcomings in its efforts.

Establishment of Wildlife Intelligence Bureaus/ Anti-Poaching Squads: The rising international trade in Wildlife and Wildlife articles has adversely impacted upon the fauna of the State. The involvement of drug traffickers and other international racketeers has aggravated the situation. In order to further strengthen the protection machinery, the State government has now initiated the process of establishing Wildlife Anti-poaching Squads (Intelligence Bureaus in 6 highly sensitive areas)-namely Bhopal, Jabalpur, Satna, Itarsi, Sagar and Seoni. The mission of these bureaus is to collect and collate the intelligence regarding the wildlife crime and to help the field administration in preventing the wildlife offences from happening all together. A detailed work plan enlisting the methodology and the role and the responsibilities of the bureaus has been prepared. Assistant Conservators of Forests, who will be heading these bureaus, have been posted at Jabalpur and Itarsi. Strengthening of these intelligence bureaus will take place soon. Establishment of these bureaus is helping the field staff in a greater way in combating wildlife crime.

Constitution of Tiger Foundation Society: Madhya Pradesh, with the highest tiger population, has the national as well as global responsibility to save the tiger and its habitat. As this responsibility cannot be shouldered by the state alone, people from all walks of life must join hands to protect the tiger and its habitats for the long-term survival of human beings and other life-forms.

The Madhya Pradesh government has, therefore, pioneered a novel scheme to secure support and help from public and organizations outside the government through formation of an independent organization - ' Madhya Pradesh Tiger Foundation Society', registered on January 15, 1997. The society has obtained Foreign Currently Regulation Act(FCRA) clearance and is authorised to receive donation from outside the country.

The role and functions of the Society are:

- Provide protection to threatened and endangered species (with added emphasis on tiger conservation)

- Provide help to the State Government and people in their effort to protect tiger habitats against fragmentation and destruction.
- Provide support to the state government to control poaching of wild animals
- To provide help in controlling illicit trade in body parts of tigers and products made out of body parts.
- To provide help in protection of tiger habitats and prey-base of tiger.
- To make general public aware of the need for conserving biodiversity and elicit their support for conservation of biodiversity. To seek help of mass media in achieving this objective.
- To reward those individuals (including forest department personnel) and institutions, organizations who have made special effort towards protection of tiger.
- To strengthen infrastructure required for protection of tigers in their habitats.
- To establish a data-bank necessary for tiger conservation in the office of the Chief Wildlife Warden, M.P. who is the secretary of this organization, and also to help development of a network of such data-bank.
- To take other measures through which conservation of tiger and other wildlife can be strengthened.

Madhya Pradesh Tiger Foundation Society is a non-profit making organization working towards conservation of wildlife and their habitats (with special emphasis on tiger). For details contact:

All monetary contributions must be sent through crossed cheques or Demand Drafts drawn in favour of the Secretary, Madhya Pradesh Tiger Foundations Society, Bhopal, India.

Till 31.3.2003, an amount of Rs. 26.21 lakhs was received as donation from individuals and institutions. This amount has been disbursed for carrying out specific works in various National Parks and Sanctuaries for which the donation were received. The foundation has also received twelve Maruti gypsy, 3 Bolero Campers, 1 Mahindra jeep,10 motor cycles and wireless sets, field gear for staff, for use in various protected areas of the state.

1. *Register as a Member:* In April, 2001 the Tiger Foundation Society has announced annual and life membership fees for obtaining membership of the society. The annual membership fee is Rs. 500 and life membership is Rs. 5,000. Any person, who desires to be member of M.P. Tiger Foundation Society, is advised to contact the local Conservator of Forests. Once a person becomes a member, he is provided with an identity card. The private membership permits each member a free visit to any of the protected area once in a year.
2. *How You may contribute towards Wildlife Conservation:*
    1. By becoming a member of the Tiger Foundation Society.
    2. By informing the local Wildlife Warden or the Chief Wildlife Warden about illegal activities concerning wildlife including illicit trade in wildlife.
    3. By joining the Tiger, leopard population estimation programme (training and actual field census)
    4. By actively campaigning for conservation of wildlife individually or as a group through your Nature Club.

BANDHAVGARH NATIONAL PARK

The Bandhavgarh National Park lies in the very heart of Madhya Pradesh and nestles blissfully among the majestic Vindhya hills. This area used to belong to the Maharaja of Rewa who handed it over to the government in 1968 thus leading to the formation of the park. Home to a wide variety of flora and fauna, the Bandhavgarh National Park sprawls across an area of 448 sq km with a huge number of extensions being dome in 1982. Covered mainly by Sal trees and bamboos, the Bandhavgarh National Park is now one of the most famous wildlife sanctuaries in the world that also boasts of a huge international profile.

The Bandhavgarh National Park came under the Project Tiger programme in 1993 and has since been one of the most visited wildlife destinations by tourists across the globe. The forests of Bandhavgarh teem with animals and birds of many types. However, the most important resident of the Bandhavgarh National Park happens to be the tiger. In fact, the Bandhavgarh National Park boasts of the highest population of tigers in India. Besides, the national park is also home to many other species like the gaur, many varieties of deer, striped hyena, jungle cat, sloth bear and many varieties of birds.

Once a hunting reserve of the royals, the Bandhavgarh National Park also used to boast of the regal white tiger. Unfortunately, they don't inhabit the park any more. Another interesting facet of Bandhavgarh is that it is the very place where author Rudyard Kipling was inspired to write his famous novel, the Jungle Book. As you explore the environs of the Bandhavgarh National Park get transported into a wonderful realm where you can view nature at its wildest best. Surely, this thrilling experience would always be present in the portals of your memory long after it is gone.

KANHA NATIONAL PARK

Located in the Mandla district of Madhya Pradesh, the Kanha National Park is one of the very first wildlife sanctuaries to come under the Project Tiger programme. This wildlife reserve extends over an entire area of 1,940 sq km and is one of the most well-known wildlife sanctuaries in the world. The entire area of Kanha is made up of a series of plateaus that stretch across the eastern segment of the majestic Satpura Range in Madhya Pradesh. Speaking of its vegetation, the Kanha National Park is mainly covered by Sal trees and extensive grasslands.

The Kanha National Park boasts of a rich variety of flora and fauna that attracts thousands of visitors around the year. In fact, it is a treat to watch the entire wildlife populace of the Kanha National Park in their jungle glory. As you navigate your way through the marked trails, get lost in a realm that exists in a state of blissful unawareness in spite of the ravages of time and commercialization. The magical glory of wilderness just lives on at the Kanha National Park.

A tour of the Kanha National Park would bring you quite close to some of its most famous residents. They include the tiger, sloth bear, tiny mouse deer, macaque, porcupines, gaur, the rare barasingha and so on. The avian population is also well represented at the Kanha National Park. They include the racquet tailed drongo, crimson breasted barbet, golden oriole and the crested eagle hawk. Besides enjoying jeep rides into the park, you can also indulge in thrilling elephant rides during your trip to the Kanha National Park. However, it must be mentioned that there are some specified timings for visitors to gain entry into the park.

PENCH NATIONAL PARK

The Pench National Park is situated on the border of Madhya Pradesh and Maharashtra and is known for the rich flora and fauna it abounds in. The park was named after the river that flows nearby and has been a protected area since 1983. Besides, the Pench National Park is also a part of the Project Tiger programme that was initiated to protect the fast dwindling tiger population.

The Pench National Park spreads over an area of 758 sq km and is mainly covered by deciduous forests. Situated near the southern reaches of the Satpura range, the Pench National Park mainly consists of small hills and an undulating terrain. The wilds of the Pench National Park abound in a variety of animals that include the tiger, wild dog, Nilgai, muntjac, gaur, the four horned antelope and the wild pig.

The Pench National Park is also home to birds like barbets, minivets, orioles, wagtails, blue kingfishers, mynahs and so on. It must also be mentioned that the Pench National Park has another attraction that amazes visitors. Well, it is the 'Kullu Tree' that grows in abundance in the region. It is a type of a gum tree that is conspicuous by its white bark.

The Pench National Park is indeed a great place to visit as part of your wildlife tour to Madhya Pradesh. As you revel in the glory of the jungle and its wild beauty, you surely feel a strange sense of communion with everything around you. Believe us, the Pench National Park adds up to a truly wonderful experience.

PANCHMARHI NATIONAL PARK

Panchmarhi in Madhya Pradesh is one of the most picturesque regions you can ever come across in the entire state. Lush greenery, cascading waterfalls and forested hills make up this wonderful region that can truly be called a favorite with nature. In fact, nature could not have been kinder going by the immense beauty it has gifted to the region. The Panchmarhi National Park is a part of this beautiful region that has never failed to mesmerize its visitors.

With a rich variety of flora and fauna to boast of, the Panchmarhi National Park is one of the most interesting places you can visit during your wildlife tour to Madhya Pradesh. As you explore the Panchmarhi National Park you will soon be enveloped by a spell that would charm you for life. You will also come across some of the most exotic animals and birds during your tour of the Panchmarhi National Park. Some of them include the tiger, panther, sambhar, chital, Nilgai and so on. It would indeed be a memorable experience to view these animals from close quarters as they bask in their jungle glory.

The Panchmarhi National Park is an artwork of nature with numerous hills, valleys, rivulets and waterfalls adorning it. The Panchmarhi National Park is mainly covered with sal, teak, tendu and bamboo trees besides a variety of grasses and medicinal plants.

Truly, a visit to the Panchmarhi National Park adds up to an experience worth living at least once in a lifetime. Castle and King invites you to be a part of this amazing experience that would fix itself in the portals of your memory forever.

8

Population and Religion

POPULATION OF MADHYA PRADESH

Madhya Pradesh is a state located in Central India. The capital city is Bhopal and Indore is the biggest city. Nicknamed the core of India in view of its geographical range in India, Madhya Pradesh is the second biggest state in the country as far as zone.

With more than 75 million inhabitants, it is the fifth biggest state in the country by population. It fringes Uttar Pradesh, Gujarat, Maharashtra and Rajasthan. Prior to the year 2000, When Chhattisgarh was under Madhya Pradesh it was the biggest state in the country. The state has a name of its own for the different types of delicious foods made here for people with different tastes.

With more than 75 Million people according to 2011, the number of tribal's in Madhya Pradesh was 12,233,000, constituting 20.27% of the aggregate population.

Talking about population, in order to check out the population of Madhya Pradesh in 2018, we need to have a look at the population of the past 5 years. They are as per the following:

1. 2013 – 74.7 Million
2. 2014 – 75.9 Million

3. 2015 – 76.4 Million
4. 2016 – 77.9 Million
5. 2017 – 78.812 Million

Predicting the 2018 population of Madhya Pradesh is not easy but we can get the idea after analysing the population from the year 2013 – 17.

As we have seen that every year the population increases by approximate 0.8224 Million people. Hence, the population of Madhya Pradesh in 2018 is forecast to be 78.812 Million + 0.8224 Million = 79.6344 Million. So, the population of Madhya Pradesh in the year 2018 as per estimated data = 79.6344 Million.

Madhya Pradesh Population 2018 –79.6344 Million. (estimated).

Demography Of Madhya Pradesh

The official language is Hindi. In addition, Urdu and Marathi are spoken by a critical number of the population since it was home to a couple of crucial and lofty Maratha states.

The state in reality has the most number of Marathi individuals outside Maharashtra. According to the assessment of 2001, 91.1% of the occupants follow Hinduism, while others are Muslim (6.4%), Jain (0.7%), Christians (0.3%), Buddhists (0.3%) and Sikhs (0.2%).

Population Density And Growth Of Madhya Pradesh

The population density of Madhya Pradesh is 230 persons per square kilometre. The population growth rate is monstrous of around 24% yearly. Every year the state by and large adds around a million people to its kitty. It is a standout among the most populated states in the nation and the pattern of the growing population at a quick rate is set to proceed in the coming years. With a convergence of individuals from different states moving here for work and other related things, there has been an expansion in the relocation numbers too of the state.

Facts About Madhya Pradesh:

1. The state experiences sub-tropical climatic conditions. Hot dry summer begins from April to June and Monsoon begins from July to September.
2. Well known Bollywood actor Arjun Rampal was born in Jabalpur city. For quite a while he studied here in Model High School. He spent the beginning days of his childhood and later on moved to Delhi and Mumbai for modeling.
3. Chandrasekher Azad was born in Madhya Pradesh. He was from a Brahmin Tiwari family and impacted the world in the Indian freedom battle.
4. Popular lyricist in Indian Film Industry Javed Akhtar is from Gwalior. Later on he went to Aligarh and Lucknowfor higher studies.
5. Madhya Pradesh is in like manner called the Heart of India in perspective of its topographical region. The genuine meaning of the state is Central Province.

DEMOGRAPHICS

Population

The population of Madhya Pradesh consists of a number of ethnic groups and tribes, castes and communities, including the indigenous tribals and relatively more recent migrants from other states. The scheduled castes and the scheduled tribes constitute a significant portion of the population of the State. The main tribal groups in Madhya Pradesh are Gond, Bhil, Baiga, Korku, Bhadia (or Bhariya), Halba, Kaul, Mariya, Malto and Sahariya. Dhar, Jhabua and Mandla districts have more than 50 percent tribal population. In Khargone, Chhindwara, Seoni, Sidhi, Singrauli and Shahdol districts 30–50 percent population is of tribes. According to the 2011 census, the adivasi population in Madhya Pradesh was 73.34 million, constituting 21.1% of the total population. There were 46 recognised Scheduled Tribes and three of them have been identified as "Special Primitive Tribal Groups" in the State.

Due to the different linguistic, cultural and geographical environment, and its peculiar complications, the diverse tribal world of Madhya Pradesh has been largely cut off from the mainstream of development. Madhya Pradesh ranks very low on the Human Development Index value of 0.375 (2011), which is below the national average. According to the India State Hunger Index (2008) compiled by the International Food Policy Research Institute, the malnutrition situation in Madhya Pradesh was "extremely alarming", receiving a severity rating between Ethiopia and Chad. The state ranks is also the worst performer in India, when it comes to female foeticides. The state's per-capita gross state domestic product(nominal GDP) is the fourth lowest in the country (2010–11). MP is also the lowest-ranked state on the India State Hunger Index.

Madhya Pradesh is one of the worst-affected states as far as malnutrition is concerned. The recent National Family Health Survey 2015–16 points out that Panna has 43.1 per cent stunted children, 24.7 per cent wasted and 40.3 per cent underweight children. Similar was the case in rural Chhatarpur where 44.4 per cent children are stunted, 17.8 per cent wasted and 41.2 per cent underweight, as per the report.

RELIGION

According to the census of 2011, 90.9% of the MP residents followed Hinduism, while others are Muslim (6.6%), Jain (0.8%), Buddhists (0.3%), Christians (0.3%), and Sikhs(0.2%).

Religion in Madhya Pradesh (2011)

Hinduism (90.89%)

Islam (6.57%)

Other religion (0.83%)

Jainism (0.78%)

Buddhism (0.30%)

Christianity (0.29%)

No religion (0.13%)

Sikhism (0.20%)

9

Art, Architecture, Fair and Festivals

ARTS AND CRAFTS OF MADHYA PRADESH

Apart from the lush forests, exuberant festivity, blissful solitude and magnificent monuments, this state located in the central part of the country of India is known for its rich tradition and culture, which gets reflected from the different works of art and craft.

Handicrafts in Madhya Pradeshportray painstaking craftsmanship and hereditary skills of the inhabitants as well as add a unique charm to the state's culture. Those artistic pieces of crafts work include woven cotton or silk sarees, fabrics with block prints, stuffed toys, floor coverings, bamboo work, cane work, jute work, woodcraft, iron craft, stone craft, metal craft, terracotta, zari work, folk paintings, ornaments, dolls and papier mache.

Most famous forms of arts and crafts of Madhya Pradesh

The state of Madhya Pradesh has got numerous forms of handicrafts as mentioned earlier. However, some of the most popular among them are as follows:

Bamboo and Cane Work

Bamboo and cane, a significant part of the rural life, is hugely used to manufacture utility articles like baskets, fishing traps, agricultural implements, hunting tools and many more. The community manufacturing and selling these handcrafted items in weekly bazaars are called as Basod or Basor. The tribal communities of Baiga, Gond and Korku are involved in this craft as well. The skilled craftsmen of the areas like Balaghat, Bastar, Chhattisgarh, Mandla, Shahdol and Seoni have harmonized their traditional techniques and knowledge to prepare new designed crafted goods to meet the modern requirements.

Carpets

Gwalior is known for carpet weaving since Mughal era. Mandla and Shahdol joined this world of craft later. Apart from being masters of carpet weaving, the craftsperson's of these areas excel in dyeing. Knotted carpets require emphasis on patterns. Vibrant woolen carpets with geometric and floral designs are an important crafted product. These designs are a blend of ancestral motifs and modern taste.

Durries

This is a kind of thick floor covering made of cotton, which is mainly manufactured in Sironj, Jabalpur, Jhabua, Raigarh and Shahdol. Woolen durries are available though. Durries are mostly prepared by rural women using the 'Punja' technique. Designed in bold patterns, these bright colored floor coverings have become a part of contemporary home decor.

Folk Paintings

This form of art of Madhya Pradesh has mainly gained its fame from the areas of Bundelkhand, Chhattisgarh, Malwa, Gondwana and Nimar. These paintings reflect the socio-cultural life of the areas. Paintings of local festivals are made of home-made colors by women. However, Bundelkhand has got a group of professional painters known as Chiteras. Painters of Chhattisgarh use mud plaster as the base of their paintings, on which patterns are engraved by fingers. This process is famously known as "Lipai". Women belonging to the Badi community of this region are famous for making tattoo. The tribal community of the Bhilala and Bhils usually paints myths, which is famous as Pithora paintings. The Malwa, Tanwarghar and Nimar regions are known for Mandana floor and wall paintings. The specialty of this painting is that drawings are made with white color on a base made out of a mixture of cow dung and red clay.

Iron Craft

Craftsmen from the interiors of the state use iron to create inimitable forms of crafts. Bhatra, Dhruva, Gond and Muria tribes offer gifts like iron made horses, trishuls etc. to God post their wish fulfillment. A traditional custom even includes gifting carved "Deeyas" on the wedding of daughters. Besides tribal statues, they prepare iron goods like candle stands, furniture, lattice, lamps and several other kinds of decorative items.

Jute Works

Jute, the second cheapest textile fiber is widely used for packaging industrial and agricultural products. Apart from its coarse character and heavy texture, the natural color increases its unique charm. Jute items like baskets, hanging lamps, flower vases, hammocks, swings, purses, footwear, table mats etc. are some of the major jute works of Bhopal, Gwalior, Indore and Raipur.

Metal Craft

Metal craft in Madhya Pradesh is a signature of the excellent and spontaneous creative skill of the tribal people. When you hold a piece in your hand you will feel the pulse with which these people make it. Go to the tribal villages of the state, you will be always hearing the iron smith's hammer going clang-clang in every little hut. The Gadhavs of Bastar, are far away from the world of modern civilization and are thereby blessed with simplicity and unique values of life. They create the marvelous metal craft which constitute a mark of their tradition.

There is another very interesting aspect of the metal craft of Madhya Pradesh. This particular craft is so popular amongst the tribal people that it has evolved a keen relationship with their faith and religion. It has become a tradition among the Gond, Muria, Bhatra and Dhruva tribals to offer iron horses, swings, trishuls (trident, the symbol of the Hindu god Shiva) to gods whenever their wishes are fulfilled. Metal crafts form a part of their social rituals also. Exquisitely carved diyas are taken by the bride along with her while going to the in laws house for the first time. They believe that doing so will bring prosperity to the husbands house and hence happiness to the newly married girl. These metal crafts known as dhokra work are mostly hollow-cast. They are made by the lost-wax process. The blacksmiths of the southern Madhya Pradesh make a range of oil lamps, tools and statues that depict animals, birds and men.

Ornaments

Have you ever seen a tribal girl adorned with ornaments in Madhya Pradesh. This is a really delightful sight. It seems as all of their joy and spirit are evoked through their jewelry. Her ornaments would include big ear and nose rings along with the heavy metallic bangles in arms as well as feet. They often wear waste bands. All sorts of ornaments are loving to the hearts of the tribals in the state of Madhya Pradesh. They intricately and artistically twist the thread to round or octahedronal metal beads and use them in making their ornaments. They sometimes weave cotton thread into a broad band to form a textured or designed base and usually then loop in buttons, beads or metallic droplets. The ornaments made of silver are a delight to the people living in the state of Madhya Pradesh. Whenever you visit a marriage ceremony you will find ladies wearing gorgeous silver ornaments which is often a mark of their respective prosperity and wealth. Silver adornments are also exhibited during the festivals.

Papier Mache

Paper mache is a peculiar craft practiced in Madhya Pradesh since very ancient times. The craft has manifested itself in various different forms. The place called Ujjain in Madhya Pradesh is famous for the production of the unique art of paper mache. However it is also practiced in various other parts of the state which include Gwalior, Bhopal and Ratlam. The art of creating objects with paper mache is very simple yet wondrous. You can easily make a stunning piece of your own from the material available in your home. This is also true with the people of the Nagvanshi community in Madhya Pradesh. From times immemorial they are making small objects with paper mache. This gradually paved the path towards the evolution of one of the finest art of the region. The people here are also engaged in the art of making mud toys and dolls. The age long expression of this craft of paper mache was in the making of the ornate objects like vases, figurines and icons. As the days are passing by, craftspersons in Bhopal and Gwalior have started on their way to make statues, birds, animals and decorative panels.

Stone Carving

Stone carving is one of the oldest form of art and crafts of Madhya Pradesh. Stone sculptures of Khajuraho, Vidisha's rock-cut temples and the monuments in Gwalior and Orchha prove the prevalence of stone carvings during the historical times. Every region of this state has got their unique and distinct style. Lattice (Jaal) work is the specialty of Gwalior whereas, Tikamgarh and Jabalpur specializes in decorative pieces of work like animals and human statues. The region of Bastar creates memorial stone pillars as well as statues of gods and goddesses of the tribal communities.

Stuffed Toys

If you ever go to Madhya Pradesh in India you will find

a spectacular art of making stuffed leather toys which is very popular. It is a typical form of handicraft in which the art objects are made according to the shapes of mostly the animals. You must be seeing the wild horses in the emporiums with hard structures and leather finish.

These are the stuffed leather toys. As the name suggests, they are covered with leather and stuffed inside with different materials which often varies according to the choice of the craftsman as well as the purpose of the toy making. It all depends upon the stuff, whether a toy will be a soft, moderate or a hard one.

The stuffed leather toys of Madhya Pradesh, looks so nice that the tourists are very much attracted and delighted, especially those who come here from the foreign countries. The expertize with which the craftsmen impart forms in these toys certainly deserves appreciation. The toys are skillfully crafted with much experienced hands and an eye for perfection. These arts are usually practiced in a hereditary way.

Terracotta

The terracotta pottery of Madhya Pradesh is marvelous in its style and representation. The potteries made by the tribal people of Bastar are really noteworthy.

These people are far from the complications of the modern civilization. They are thereby blessed with simplicity and deep realization of the basic values of life system along with an enormous respect towards their deities and rituals. The art of terracotta marks the first human attempt of craftsmanship. This is why this art is so popular amongst the aboriginals of the country. Traditional statues of elephants, serpents, birds as well as horses from Bastar are unique in their style. There is an interesting practice among the tribes. They often offer the terracotta pieces depicting different animals to the local deity in lieu of sacrifice.

Textile Weaving

Madhya Pradesh, also known as the "heart of India", is

famous for its extensive history of textiles. From seventh century BC to second century BC, old age scripts mention Madhya Pradesh as a prominent hub of textile weaving. The most famous textile products in Madhya Pradesh include the Chanderi and Maheshwari Sarees. The handicrafts of Madhya Pradesh are a reflection of the rich culture and tradition of this state. The type of raw materials that are implemented might have changed throughout the years and the usage of the products manufactured has also changed but an extensive history of textile industries in the state keeps on contributing to the extremely unique handicrafts industry of the state.

Woodcraft

Woodcraft is a traditional art of India as also of Madhya Pradesh. It strikingly exhibits a person's efficiency and imagination which can transform a simple log of wood into a marvelous object of art. The works of woodcraft are predominant in various parts of Madhya Pradesh. Whenever you go to the state never ever forget to notice the intricately embellished wooden ceilings, doors as well as lintels. They are adorned with nicely carved patterns. These excellent craftsmanship indicates the rich traditional heritage of this sphere of art in the central part of the country.

Woodcraft in Madhya Pradesh exhibits the traditional art of amazingly beautiful wooden handicrafts. These woodcrafts are employed both for utilitarian as well as architectural purposes.

Zari Embroidery

The art of zari work is centered around Bhopal, the capital city of Madhya Pradesh which is known for its rich heritage of art and craft. The art is predominant here for the last 300 years. Apart from Bhopal, it is practiced widely in Gwalior and Indore. The zari work in Madhya Pradesh has come from the western part of the country. This industry witnessed the glorious days of the great emperors. All the rulers were great patrons of art and architecture. They had an intense respect and passion for Indian traditional art especially those belonging to the central part of the peninsula.

The rulers of Madhya Pradesh had a passion for grandeur. This might be the reason why they got inclined towards the zari work. The members of the royal family were dressed with the priceless works of zari. You can witness the royal dresses if you go to the royal museums, especially to the museums at Bhopal, Gwalior and Indore.

ARCHITECTURE

Madhya Pradesh – Explore The Heart of India

Hindustan Ka Dil Dekho – Explore the magnificent uniqueness of the heart of India "Incredible Madhya Pradesh". M. P. is a state lies at center of India,It was the biggest Indian state before 2000.

It ranks among the most popular tourist attractions in India for its wonderful ancient Indian architecture. The Tribal state has many tourist attraction such as Khajuraho, Sanchi stupa,Upper lake, Bhimbeta and Pachmarhi.

Apart from the above major attraction it also offers a wide range of flora and fauna,which includes the great cats, leopard, wild langur and other wild animals. The city of lakes Bhopal is the capital of the Madhya Pradesh and also counted as one of the greenest city in India.

Indore ,Bhopal, Gwalior And Jabalpur are considered as the four metro cities of the state. Each city is famous for its unique culture and traditions, Indore is well famous for foods items.

Best Places to See in Madhya Pradesh

Khajuraho: Most visited tourist destinations in Madhya Pradesh is Khajuraho,The Fascinating Temples of Love in India. Temples of Khajuraho are well famous in the world for its erotic Sculptures. Its sculptured temples dedicated to Lord Shiva, Among the temples of Khajuraho, The kandariya mahadeo temple is the largest and the grandest one, this is one of the most visited temple among the group of monuments in Khajuraho, Madhya Pradesh.

Orchha: Orcha, one of the ancient city situated on the bank of river Betwa. This place is famous for Raja Ram Temple,Orchha Palace, Chhatris and various other historical monuments. The Bundelkhand region of India is one of the most beautiful and hidden wealth of Madhya Pradesh, apart from the photos of graceful monuments, one can also click the picture of beautiful woman carrying water pot on her head.

Sanchi Stupa: Sanchi is a small village in Raisen District. The Sanchi stupa in Sanchi, Madhya Pradesh built by Emperor Ashoka the Great in the third century BC. The Sanchi Stupa is one of the best preserved early stupas in central India, surrounded by a railing with four carved gateways facing all the four directions.

Bhimbetka: The Rock Shelters of Bhimbetka are situated in the foothills of the Vindhya mountain range,near Raisen bhopal. Bhimbetka have a number of interesting paintings which depict the lives and times of the people who lived in the caves. The Rock Shelters of Bhimbetka are a recognized world heritage site by UNESCO.

Bagh Caves: The Bagh Caves are a group of nine rock-cut monuments situated on Vindhyas range in Dhar district of Madhya Pradesh. These are the Buddhist caves and a great architecture of Indian rock-cut architecture.

Bhojpur: It is very famous for temple of lord Shiva, situated near to Bhopal. The temple has the largest Shiva lingam in India. Bhojpur also has an unfinished Jain temple.

Omkareshwar: Omkareshwar,is on an island called Mandhata or Shivapuri in the Narmada river,situated in Khandwa district. It is one of the 12 revered Jyotirlinga shrines of Lord Shiva.The sacred island, shaped like the holiest of all Hindu symbols "Om". Omkareshwar is one of the sacred places in the state of Madhya Pradesh.

Ujjain: Ujjain, one of the oldest city in India situated on the bank of Holy river Shipra. Ujjain is famous for MahakaleshwarJyotirlinga, one of the most famous Hindu temples dedicated to Lord Shiva. The temple is situated on the side of the Rudra Sagar lake.Ujjain also host the biggest fair of India the Great "Kumbh mela".

FAIRS AND FESTIVALS

Fairs can be called the panorama of culture of Madhya Pradesh and its colour ful life style. Economically, socially and culturally, these fairs show a unique and rare combination which is not found elsewhere.

The maximum number of fairs, if we look at them district wise numbering 227 are held in Ujjain district and the lowest number i.e., 13 fairs only are held in Hoshangabad district.

Most of the fairs are held during the months of March, April and May when the farmers have less work to do in the fields. June, July, August and September are the lazy months for the fairs as the farmers are busy during the rainy season.

Here is a brief information about some of these fairs:

Simhastha

Kumbha in Ujjain known as Simhastha, is a grand and one of the holiest fairs of the country. It has got very high religious values and is held here in a cycle of every twelve years when Jupiter enters the Leo sign of the zodiac known as Simha Rashi. On the bank of the holy river Kshipra, Simhastha is held with all its grand paraphernalia and millions of people from whole of the world gather here for their spiritual elevation. In fact, apart from its importance, in terms of being the venue for Simhastha, the ancient city Ujjain enjoys the reputation of having one of the twelve Jyotirlingas of India. The city takes pride in being a great seat of learning when Lord Krishna and his friend Sudama were taught by Guru Sandipani Rishi here. It is also a land of the great poet Kalidas and the saints like Sandipani and Bhartrihari.

Aalami Tableegi Ijtima

This three-day congregation is considered among the most important religious occasions celebrated in Bhopal. Ijtima is held every year and is accompanied by a fair. When the event takes place, a gust of spirituality prevails over the city and Muslims from all over the globe in 'Jamaats' (group of Devotees) descend here. 'Jamaatis' from the countries like Russia, Kazakhstan, France, Indonesia, Malaysia, Zambia, South Africa, Kenya, Iraq, Saudi Arab, Yemen, Ethiopia, Somalia, Turkey, Thailand and Sri Lanka arrive here to camp for three days and listen to the holy sermons of Islamic scholars on how to lead conscientious and upright life by following good values. The event also holds special religious discourses for intellectuals, students, traders, farmers etc. with underlying message of universal brotherhood.

This conclave is considered to be one of the largest religious congregations in the world and disseminates spiritual messages, which are relevant to not just the Muslims but for all communities.

Fair Of Ramlila

This fair is organised in the Bhander Tehsil of Gwalior district. It is more than 100 years old. January-February are the months reserved for it.

Fair of hira bhumia

The name of Hiraman Baba is famous in Gwalior, Guna and nearby areas. It is believed that Hiraman Baba's blessings remove the barrenness of women. This fair is held in the months of August and September in the entire region as Hira Bhumia fairs.

Fair Of Pir Budhan

More than 250 years old, this fair is held in Sanwara of Shivpuri district near the tomb of the Muslim saint Pir Budhan. The time for holding this fair is in August-September.

Fair Of Nagaji

In November – December, this fair is organised in the memory of Nagaji saint who lived during the period of Akbar. It is held in the Porsa village of Morena district for about a month. Previously, monkeys were sold here but now other domestic animals have also been added to them.

Fair Of Tetaji

Tetaji was a truthful man. It is said, that he had been given the power to remove the snake venom from the body. This fair is held on the birthday of Tetaji for the last 70 years in the Bhamavad village of Guna district.

Fair Of Jageshwari Devi

This fair is held in Chanderi of Guna district since time immemorial. There is an anecdote that the ruler of Chanderi was a devotee of Jageshwari Devi. He had leprosy. Devi asked him to come to a place after 15 days. But Raja arrived there on the third day only. At that time only the head of Devi appeared. His leprosy was cured and from that day this fair started.

Amarkantak Shivratri Fair

At the origin of river Narmada in Amarkantak of Shahdol district, a fair is held during the Shivratri day for the last eighty years.

Fair Of Mahamrityunjay

There is a temple of Mahamrityunjay in Rewa where fairs are held every year on Basant Panchami and Shivratri.

Fair Of Chandi Devi

At Ghoghara village in Sidhi district is a temple of Chandi Devi who is believed to be the incarnation of goddess Parvati. This fair is held during March-April.

Urs Of Baba Shahabuddin Aulia

In February at Neemuch of Mandsaur district, this Urs is celebrated for 4 days. There is the shrine of Baba Shahabuddin.

Fair Of Kaluji Maharaj

This fair is held for a month in Pipalyakhurd of West Nimar. It is said that some 200 years ago Kaluji Maharaj used to cure the diseases of human beings and animals by his power.

Fair Of Singaji

Singaji was an esoteric man and was respected as a deity. This fair is held for a week in August-September in Pipalya village of West Nimar.

Dhamoni Urs

This fair is held in April-May at Dhamoni in Sagar district on the shrine of Mastan Shah Vali.

Fair Of Barman

This 13 days fair starts from Makar Sankranti in Gadarwara of Narsinghpur district.

Fair Of Math Ghoghara

This 15 days fair is held in Bhaironthan of Seoni district on Shivratri. A natural lake and a cave beautify this place.

Khajuraho Festival of Dances

The world renowned temple town of Khajuraho in Madhya Pradesh designated by UNESCO as a world heritage site for its archaeological and historical monuments, draws crowds from India and abroad to a culturally enriched show of classical dances in the months of February-March. An internationally recognized festival of classical dances, Khajuraho dance festival in the city known for the fabulous architecture of its temples built by Chandelas is an attempt by the organiser Madhya Pradesh Kala Parishad, to contribute towards promotion of cultural heritage of the nation.

The exponents of the popular classical dance forms are invited from every part of the country to perform during this week long festival. Classical Indian dance forms like Kathak,

Kuchipudi, Odissi, Bharatnatyam, Manipuri, Mohiniattam are performed by outstanding exponents. The strength of tradition and spirituality gives the performance an unusual and attractive appeal. Classical Hindustani music is used for accompaniment in most of these dance forms. It is considered to be a privilege by the exponents of classical Indian dancers to perform during the Khajuraho Dance Festival.

Lokrang Festival

The five day long festival of Lokrang in Bhopal begins every year on 26th January, the Republic day. It is a cultural exposition organised by Madhya Pradesh Adivasi Lok Kala Academy. The efforts are to bring the performing and creative aspects of the culture of folk and tribal people from the entire nation. The main features of the Lokrang are folk and tribal dances, classical dances, performing art forms. Exhibitions and presentations from abroad are also a big draw.

Lokranjan Festival

Organised by Madhya Pradesh Tourism Department, Lokranjan is a national festival of folk dances held at Khajuraho every year. The activities include presentation of popular folk and tribal dance forms from various parts of India and a craft bazaar to exhibit and demonstrate the creations of the traditional artisans. This festival in the heritage city of Khajuraho is a magnificent spectacle, as it unveils the majesty and grandeur of a world famed temple site and provides an opportunity to catch up the colour and creativity of the tribal and rural life style.

IMPORTANT FAIRS AND FESTIVALS

Madhya Pradesh has a list of innumerable fairs and festivals including all the common major occasions. Existing rituals and collective behaviour have cast their impressions by diffusing certain practices with traditions.

Fairs: The popular fairs occur mostly in the months of Phalguna, Chaitra, Bhadra, Asvina and Kartika. During

Phalguna many fairs coincide with the Holi and Shivaratri. The Tansen Urs also falls at Gwalior during this season. Sankranti Melas are held at various places. Melas held around Basant Panchami are also important. Baldeviji Ka Mela (Panna), Rajim Mela and the fairs held in Bilaspur district are worth notice.

In the tribal villages of Bastar the **Madai fairs** record their social consideration as of vital importance to all the ethnic groups of the area. The Madai fairs of Narayanpur, Kondagaon, Dantewara and Dhanara, falls within February, March and April every year.

In the **Chaitra fair** held at Biaora (Malwa), the Dhup Dehi ka Mela of Hirapur (Rewa Division), the Ram Navami fair of Naya Gaon, the Bhilat Baba ka Mela of Seoni and the Gal Yatras held at over two dozen villages of Malwa are worth mention.

A good number of fairs are held in the 10th day of the month of Bhadra, to mark the birth of Tejaji. Many tales are current about this legendary figure. In **Tejaji's fairs** rituals are made to cure snake-bite. In Guna district at Bhamavad village there is a platform on which a statue of Tejaji on his horse is installed. Every year during the fair many persons come with pieces of cloth round their necks. This they untie near the platform and as soon as they untie it, they become unconscious only to regain it after water and milk are sprinkled on their faces. Similar rituals are witnessed in the fairs held at Sagar village of the same area and at Rawati of Ratlam district.

In the months of Asadha and Bhadra, at Deotalab (Rewa) the Somnath Sankarji ka Mela and Tejaji fair draw thousands of people. The Triveni ka Mela held at Ratlam and the Singaji Jatra held at Piplya vilage of Nimad encourage the people to attend fairs occurring in Kartika at Ujjain, Mandhata (Nimad), Naya Gaon and many other places. The Kumbha Mela is held after every twelve years at Ujjain.

Lachhandas Baba's fair (Laljit ka Pura-Morena) or the fairs of Hira Bhumia (Gird-Gwalior), Shah Peer Budhan (Sanwarw-Shivapuri district), Abda Peer (Bamhori-Rewa), Chaumukh

Nath (Panna), Baba Shabuddin Saheb Oulia (Mandsaur district), Kaluji Maharaj (Piptya Khurd-West Nimad) and Singaji (Rajpur Tehsil-Nimad), Khalari (Mahasamund-Raipur) etc., carry a number of anecdotes about their beginning. Bhilat Baba ka Mela (Malapur and Seoni Malwa-Hoshangabad), Garibnath Baba ka Mela (Awantipur Barodia-Shajapur district) and Kana Baba ka Mela (Harda Tehsil) have many legends behind them. Ramlila Mela of Bhander is one of the oldest fair supposed to be over a century old. The Bhaya Sokar Devi fair of Rewa, the Unao or Baramju fair of Datia are also old fairs. The Somhar Dev Baba ka Mela of Goradiya village (West Nimad) is held in the honour of Somhar Dev whose glory is recited in a narrative called Pathwad.

Festivals: The festivals observed by all the classes living in the state are Dussehra, Diwali, Holi and Ganesh Chaturthi. Other festivals common to non-tribals are Basant Panchami, Nag Panchami, Janmashtami, Shivaratri and Ram Navami. For the tribes, the Bhils and the Gonds, every festival is followed by some sort of animal sacrifice. The tribals of Bastar often complement their economy by community hunts like Pandum and Parad.

Gana-Gour: Gana-gour which is the festival of the north-western regions of Madhya Pradesh is celebrated in honour of Shiva and Parvati. 'Gana' means Shiva and 'Gour' means Parvati or Rano Bai.

Rano Bai's parental house was in Malwa and she was married in Rajasthan. Rano Bai was a beloved child of her parents and she was so much attached to Malwa that she did not like staying in Rajasthan with her husband. After marriage she could come to Malwa only once a year. Gana-Gour symbolizes the coming back of Rano Bai to her parental house after marriage.

The womenfolk of Malwa observe Gana-Gour twice a year. Once in the month of Bhadra and the other in the month of Chaitra. But the importance is given to the Chaitra Teej, *i.e.* the third day of the bright half of Chaitra (March - April). The preliminaries of the festival are started just after Holi and conclude on Chaitra Teej. The post-Holi period punctuates the changes of the season. For unmarried girls, it signalizes the arrival of puberty. Prior to the Gana-Gour day girls go to the riverside singing traditional songs, and return home with jars full of water and green leaves. The ritual is called Phul-Pati which means flowers and leaves.

The other visual aspect of the festival is the idol of Gana-Gour, which is made a week in advance. The Rawat women of Chhattisgarh prepare idols of both Shiva and Parvati and call the pair Isar-Gair. The Gonds make an idol of Bhimsen along with that of Isar-Gour. Different classes of Hindus prepare the idols according to their own age-old fashion. The war-loving tribes adore the idol of Shiva with a sword in one hand and a shield on the back.

The Gana-Gour festival includes offering of grown wheat or blades of rice to the idols by married women. The ritual is made for the blossoming of married life and the welfare of the community. In Surguja district, after completing the ceremonial rituals women dance the Karna which lasts the whole night. In Malwas the puja is performed daily in the evening till the concluding day. It follows the traditional dance around the idol. The dance is extremely simple. It consists of circular movements round the images of Gana-Gour. All such performances are arranged in the houses with large courtyards. At the end sugar-bubbles, (batasha) are distributed among the gathering by the host. On the last day of the festival, the idols are led out in procession to bid ceremonial farewell at river-banks or tanks. The Gana-Gour of the Dhakars are taken out in procession with the beating of drums and the playing of musical instruments.

Gana-Gour is repeated on the third day of Bhadra in the form of Kajli Teej to confirm the setting in of the rainy season. Swings are put on all the big trees of the village. A festive look is given to the houses and songs are once again echoed. In Chhattisgarh lyrics are sung in praise of goddess Durga and Mother Sharda. The sentiments of newly-married girls also find expression in may of the songs. The festival corresponds with the Gavar of Rajasthan. Gaura is a parallel festival celebrated in Chhattisgarh, the only exception being that it falls in Kartika instead of Chaitra or Bhadra.

Ganga Dashmi: The festival falls on the tenth day of the second fortnight of Jyaistha (May-June). In Surguja district, the occasion is observed by the Adivasis and the non-Adivasis. The classes of the Hindu fold celebrate it because on this day the river Ganges had its descent on the earth. They take a dip in any nearby river and make offerings. The tribals go in batches with their women to the riverside to drink and dance. Games and local competitions are arranged between both the sexes. The Adivasis take the occasion just for having a feast and fun.

Ghaila and Bidri: Ghaila is the earthen pot ceremony of the Gonds. It is a ceremony identical to the Akhadi or Akadhi (Akshya Tratiya) of the Hindus. It is performed in the month of Jyaistha (May-June). Certain rites are conducted by the village head-man and the fields are harrowed by the peasants. Then follows the sacrifice of five chickens by a Bhumia.

The sowing season begins in Gondwana with the sacrifice of a goat and Thakur Dev is propitiated in the Bidri ceremony. A feast is arranged and served to the villagers. The rites are always performed by a Baiga. This festival corresponds to the feast of transplantation of paddy seedlings celebrated by the Munda and most other settled agricultural tribes of Chhotanagpur.

Hareli or Hariri: Hareli or Hariri falls on the day of Sravana Amavasya. In Mandla, it is celebrated on the new-moon day of the same month. The festival is significant for the agriculturists of central India. On this day, all peasants and farmers offer puja to their implements. No one works the whole day. Paddy seedlings are stuck over the doors of houses by Dewar priests in Mandla villages. Men go and plant green twigs in the field with certain rites, wishing to have good crops. Anadai, the goddess of crops, is invoked to give them prosperity. Young boys give an additional touch to the occasion by display of walking and running on stilts. In Malwa, the festival is called

Harya Gondiya, with the difference that it is observed exclusively by women as Vrat, in the month of Asadha.

Kajri Navami: On the ninth day of the waxing-moon fortnight of the month of Sravana, falls the Kajri festival. In the Bundelkhandi-speaking area only those women, who are blessed with sons, observe this festival. Their worship-ritual continues till the full-moon day of the same month. This day is also recognised as Kajri Purnima and Savani. For the fisher-folk of the western coast of the country, it is an occasion for offering coconuts to the sea.

On the Sravan Shukla Navami, the women go to a particular field and bring earth from there. This is kept in leaf-cups and in these leaf-cups is sown wheat or barley. These cups are kept in the inner room of the house, devoid of air and sunrays. In the room where these cups are kept, the floor is washed with cattle-dung and a part of the wall is also coated with the cattle-dung solution. On this part a design is made with rice-solution. Figures of a house, a child in cradle, a mongoose and a woman with a pitcher are drawn near this design.

It is this folk art which is known as Navami. Due worship of this is performed before sowing the wheat or barley seedlings. Everyday the worship is repeated till the fifteenth day and in the evening of this Purnima day, the cups are taken for immersion. The ladies form a procession, each carrying the leaf-cups on her head and go singing to some tank where they are immersed. On the Kajri Navami the women keep fast.

Karam: Karam or Karma is the festival of the Oraon, Baiga, Binjhawar and Majhwar tribes. It occurs in the month of Bhadra.

The centre of the ritual consists in the cutting of three branches of Karam tree (Gonds fetch branches of Kalmi or galdu tree) and their installation in the 'akhara' or dancing ground. The branches are called the 'Karam Raja'. The entry of the branches into the village is accompanied by dancing and after the installation Karam dancers revolve round the Raja through the night. The following morning the branches are garlanded and the Karam legend is recited. Flowers are then thrown over the Raja and offerings of curd and rice are made. Red karan baskets full of grain are also put before the branches and some ceremonially nurtured barley seedlings are distributed among the boys and girls who put the yellow blades in their hair. The blessing of Karam Raja is then sought and the branches are taken up and carried by women through the village.

Girls of the Gond tribe celebrate Karam by carrying earthen pots with holes and oil lamps inside them, go from house to house, collecting eatables and coins. This is done in the month of Asvina. The Korwa and Korku Adivasis celebrate this occasion after the harvest. Karam is also associated with a variety of dances and folk songs.

Bhojali (Bhujalia): This significant festival of Chhattisgarh is observed in the month of Bhadra. About a week before the actual Bhojali day, *i.e.* on the day of Nagpanchami, wheat, gram, rice or kondo seeds are sown in earthen pots and manured to grow into green shoots. These seeds are watered everyday with a view to having the ensuing crop in abundance. The sprouting of the seeds are called Bhujaria in Bundelkhand and Jawara in Malwa. At some places seeds are nurtured in leaf-cups or 'churkus' which is a kind of conical baskets tied at the top of bamboo pieces.

On the Bhojali day, meals are held in every town, village and locality. The womenfolk of the countryside holding the Bhojali (the seedlings) in their hands or keeping the earthen pots containing the green growth on their heads go in groups to nearby rivers or tanks. There the Bhojali is floated over the water. While on the way to the river they sing ceremonial songs, many of which are addressed to the river Ganges.

In Bundelhand, blades of grain are exchanged among friends and relatives. In Chhattisgarh, during the festival, women assemble at the melas and address one another in terms of Bhojali. When the sprouts are submitted to the water, the concluding songs generally refer to Bhojali as a deity, close to the mother-goddess.

Kujlaya: On the full moon day of Bhadra, the festival of Kujlaya is celebrated to commemorate the reunion of the legendary queen, Malhana Devi, with her daughter who had been married to the son of a hostile king.

Nine days before the Kujlaya, wheat or barley is sowed in small baskets filled with black soil and manure. Then, on the full-moon day women of the locality assemble at someone's place and tie rakhi to their brothers and nearest relatives, including husbands, or would be marriage partners in case of unmarried girls. The following day the basket of wheat or barley seedlings are taken out in procession to a river side to sink their contents, except the green shoots which they distribute among themselves in the name of Malhana Devi. On way to the river they sing a few songs.

Arwa Teej: The festival is specially observed by the unmarried girls in Chhattisgarh and it is held during the month of Vaisakha. The occasion is marked by making a small canopy of mango twigs, decorated according to individual taste. This whole thing is a dress rehearsal for marriage and is usually followed by feeding the neighbours. Special songs are sung on the occasion. The most popular songs smack of sentimental flavour which are associated with the bride's home-coming.

In some parts of Madhya Pradesh, Arwa Teej coincides with Akhateej (Akshya Tratiya) which marks the commencement of the agricultural year.

Sanja and Mamulia: Unmarried girls of north-western Madhya Pradesh annually worship a legendary girl called Sanja. The ritual is associated with figures and designs made by girls on smeared portions of mud walls through the medium of cattle-dung.

In the month of Asvina, the festivities of Sanja run consecutively for sixteen days. Everyday new designs and figures are made and in the evening songs are recited in chorus before them. Corresponding to the Sanja, the girls in Bundelkhand worship Mamulia. Mamulia is represented by a green branch of a lemon tree. The branch is adorned with a coloured skirt and a wimple. Wild flowers are attached in each thorn of the branch and dry fruits and sweets are hung around it. Music is played round the branch and later it is taken to a pond for immersion.

Ghadlya: Girls have their own feature in this festival. They gather in the evening in groups and visit every house of the village carrying earthen pots with holes for the light to come out, made by a wick oil lamp kept inside. The pot is also termed Ghadlya or Ghurla which means a horse, as it is known in Malwa.. The girls recite songs connected with Ghadlya in front of every house. In return they get foodstuff or coins. The Gond girls observe a similar festival. The boy's festival is known as Chhala. In the adjoining region of Bundelkhand, it is identified as Tesoo.

Suwata: The Suwata of Bundelkhand relates to the Ghadlya of Malwa. Girls, in this form of celebration prepare a mini platform along the wall with clay. The three sides of this platform are provided with steps. On the platform an image of a demon is made to stand. The sun and the moon are drawn on the wall to give an idea of two brothers. On the head of the demon's image, small images of both Shiva and Parvati are placed. Only these figurines are invoked. Oblation of flowers and green grass blades are made to them and songs connected with the Suwata, sung. These songs are generally attributed to Gouri, the consort of Lord Shiva.

Pandum or Parad: Confined to the Abujhmarias of Bastar, the Pandum festival is observed during the community hunt. Before starting for the hunting expedition, offerings are made by the Hill Marias for a rich game and the safe return of the hunters.

In the month of Phalguna the other tribes of Bastar arrange hunting expeditions which continue for many days. Ceremonial hunts are believed to help a rich harvest of animals in the forest and a bumper crop. There are various types of Parad. Birds are hunted in the Chidayi Parad and small animals are killed in the Chotti Parad. In Beej Parad, weapons are sanctified and seeds are brought. Deities are propitiated and the nature of the hunt is predicted by Perma, the village sorcerer.

Navanna: As soon as Diwali is over, the feast of Navanna is celebrated. It depends on the full ripening of corns; only then is the day for Navanna fixed. In Bundelkhand, it is performed on the eleventh day after Diwali. On this day cows are fed with cakes prepared out of new corn. No one takes his food until this rite is done. The Gonds first of all perform offerings of green paddy to the Saj tree and then to Bhavani Mata Holera Dev (the cattle deity), Narayan Dev and Rat Mai (night mother), who is believed to live in the verandah of every house.

Chherta or Khichharahi: The festival of Chherta falls on the last day of the month of Pausa. The ploughmen cease their work on this day and all their accounts are settled as the succeeding day *i.e.* the first day of the month of Magha. This day is considered to be the new year day for opening new accounts in Chhattisgarh. Fowls and goats are sacrificed and Karma is danced the whole night.

The Gond, the Bhumia, the Panka and even the non- Adivasi boys and girls of Mandla district celebrate this festival to conclude it with a grand feast. Groups of boys and girls are formed and they go shouting from house to house. The boys collect gifts from every house. Kondo or maize, grain, kutki and whatever received by them is mixed up in a pot and cooked at a nearby river or pond. The food prepared in such a way is called Khichhari. Hence the feast of Chherta has the name Khichharahi.

When the meal gets ready a boy or a girl is chosen to act as a crow. Some food is put on a leaf-platter and placed on the ground. Then the boy or the girl acting as the crow approaches it to take the leaf-platter. At that moment all the children rush at the crow and beat it with burning faggots. The crow angrily caws at them a few times and at the convenient moment snatches the leaf-platter and runs away. After that all children sit down and eat their meal from the leaf plates. Towards evening they all return home.

Meghnad: It is a festival of the Gond tribe, usually held within the first half of Phalguna. The dates for celebrating the festival are different at different places but all falling in the first fortnight of Phalguna. At some places, Meghnad is held in the month of Chaitra. The idea of having different dates to celebrate the festival is to facilitate people of one area to go and join the people of other villages before or after propitiating Meghnad at their own places.

Meghnad is believed by the Gonds to be their supreme deity. The celebration begins immediately after the Holi festival. The main structure symbolizing Meghnad consists of a platform built on four poles. The fifth pole juts out through the platform and bears a horizontal beam easy enough to rotate freely in a circular fashion. The platform is reached through a ladder made by two connecting poles of the platform itself with wooden rafters. The structure is generally painted with red ochre and oil. All sorts of things like earthen pots with motif designs, turmeric paints, coloured strings, cock's feathers and mixed sounds are experienced in the milieu. This gives the feelings of a puja being performed. The whole structure of the Meghnad represents the Khandera Dev of the tribe. Meghnad is mainly a tribal festival.

In times of illness the people of Chhindwara remember Khandera Dev. They also remember him for bumper crops. Vows are made. Promises are uttered to offer so and so on the fulfillment of the desired things. When actual ritual is arranged coconuts, eggs, chickens and goats are ordinarily offered. Propitiators very often climb five steps of the ladder and thereby carry out the vow of Panch-Patoni. In serious troubles, they undertake the risk of swinging in the air by getting themselves tied by the waist, face downward, to one end of the revolving beam. A man on the ground holds the rope attached to the beam and moves around the structure, which is usually forty to forty-five feet in height.

As the ritual is the central attraction of the occasion, the gathering provides an atmosphere of a village fair with songs and rhythmic beats of drums and cymbals. Women get possessed by the spirit of the god Khandera and start trembling near the Meghnad platform.

Gordhan (Gobardhan): Gordhan festival is celebrated on the sixteenth day in the month of Kartika *i.e.* just on the day following Diwali. Gobardhan means 'prosperity for cows' and seems to have its origin in the Krishna cult.

On this day they decorate their cows and cattle and rub oil on their bodies and horns. The cattle are fed first of all in the morning and they are given green fodder, oil and sugar. Cows are worshipped with the respect due to a goddess.

The Bhils of Malwa sing to the cattle some anecdotal songs, known as Heeda. Figures of Gordhan are made by cow-dung on the ground and a series of earthen lamps are placed near them. Three figures are usually made, two of which are named Gordhan and the third one is called Chugalkhor Jamai (back-biter son-in-law). It is interesting that these figures are made to be crushed by the hoofs of the cattle. Women treat the day as Suhag Padwa (blessed day). While worshipping the Gordhan, women of Malwa sing the Chandrawali song, associated with Krishna's romance. The theme-structure in this song is about Chandrawali's husband, Gordhan.

The tribes like Gonds and the Bhumias play a passive part in this post-Diwali celebration. For the Ahirs, who were the cowherd community it is the day for dancing and rejoicing. They offer coconut and rice to Kher Dev, the god of grazing ground. They also paint their cattle, trim their horns with tassels and put garlands of flowers and cowries around their necks.

In some villages of Gondwana the ritual grazing of cattle is done on this day. The men who have vowed to do so for twelve consecutive years are called 'Mauniar'. During the day they must fast. They use a flute instead of a stick when driving the cattle to the grazing ground. They dress like men but wear feminine ornaments. The whole day they remain in the jungle, grazing the cattle and may return to the village before dusk. Then they hang their flutes up in the house, take off their ornaments, wash their hands and take their first meal of the day.

It is believed that a man who has done this grazing on Diwali for thirteen years will be reborn as a cow, if after his death all the ceremonies and funeral feasts are properly performed.

Bhagoriah: Bhagoriah is celebrated just after Holi, in the month of Phalguna. Bhagoriah is held for the selection of spouses. Besides fun and frolic, the festival provides opportunity for taking revenge on the enemies.

Bhagoriah starts a week before the Holi festival. Normally, it is made to coincide with the market day of a particular place. It continues for the whole week and the assemblage shifts from one place to another, adjusting with the market days of the other villages of the region.

From early morning the enthusiastic villagers will come to the market place where the Bhagoriah festival is held. Each family coming down to participate in the festival may camp at a few places from the spot where the market is to be held. They carry with them a big drum which is a major attraction in the festivities. Old men and women stay in the camp itself, allowing the unmarried boys and girls to participate in the festival.

These young people go in separate groups to and fro in the market carrying with them gulal, a red powder. While moving about, the boys smear gulal on the forehead of the girls of their choice. The girls too return their love by applying gulal on the boy's fore-heads. If a girl does not reciprocate, it indicates her disapproval to become that boy's 'ladi' (dignified woman). The willingness is confirmed by making the girl eat 'majoom' (mixture of molasses, bhang and green colour). If the girl swallows majoom, she automatically becomes his property. Now they fix up a rendezvous. Here the girl conveys her verbal consent and both go to the boy's home. News of the girl's arrival is informed to her parents and if they agree, further steps to regularise the union are taken and they become husband and wife.

The day is also considered to be a day for taking revenge. Challenge to one's enemies is made when one dances in groups at the festival.

Laru Kaj: Laru Kaj is the festival of Gonds which is associated with the pig sacrifice. The ceremony is considered the pig's wedding in honour of Narayan Dev. This sacrifice is supposed to be done by every family once in nine or twelve years for prosperity, health and happiness. All the relatives come and stay at the host's house for several days. Invitation is sent to many persons in the village to join the ceremony.

'Laru' means bridegroom and 'Kaj' refers to a 'Solemn occasion'. It also means ceremony or marriage. Nowadays, this sacrificial ritual is gradually disappearing.

Koqsar: Koqsar is one of the important festivals of the Abujhmarias. It comes as the concluding festival when people care little for privacy. Koqsar is characterised by ceremonial exchange of visits of boys and girls. In most of the Abujhmar country, this festival is associated with the end of long separation. Koqsar marks the lifting of the taboo. In Koqsar the men dance in semi-circle and the girls dance in a separate group. The dance proceeds through the whole night.

In the Bhagoriah of the Bhils, marriages are settled in Koqsar and it is after the festival that couples meet again and many boys are able to secure partners for the life ahead.

Ras-Nawa: Ras-Nawa is a special festival of the Baigas of Mandla district. Ras-Nawa means ceremonial eating of honey. The festival falls once in every nine years. The Baigas associate this festival to their legendary ancestor Nanga Baiga.

The shrubs called Mohati and Anhera are the favourites of the bees as they get ample honey out of their flowers. Once a drop of honey fell to the ground, Nanga Baiga dipped his finger and tasted the substance. No sooner he did this, all the bees transformed into tigers. Nanga Baiga ran for his life and when he reached his abode he found it filled with bees. He was unable to move either inside the house or outside. He promised to make offering every nine years.

It is believed that preceding this festival many deaths occur and therefore among the Baigas a taboo is observed not to eat honey before the festival. On the festival day the Baigas go to the forest to get honey. On their return to the village a festal booth is built for the Mohati and Anhera shrubs. They are now taken as wife and husband. Near the festal booth millet is prepared by 'Shaman', the witch doctor, in gourds and when it is ready honey is poured into the vessels. It is distributed to all those who attend the ceremony. During the merriment boys take their chances to smear the faces of the girls with honey.

10

Education

INTRODUCTION

According to the 2011 census, Madhya Pradesh had a literacy rate of 70.60%. According to the 2009–10 figures, the state had 105,592 primary schools, 6,352 high schools and 5,161 higher secondary schools. The state has 208 engineering & architecture colleges, 208 management institutes and 12 medical colleges.

Exams at the Mahatma Gandhi Seva Ashram, Jaura

The state is home to some of the premier educational and research institutions of India including Indian Institute of Science Education and Research (IISER) Bhopal, IIM Indore, IIT Indore, Maulana Azad National Institute of Technology(Bhopal), IIITDM Jabalpur and IIITM Gwalior, Indian Institute of Tourism and Travel Management, SPA

Bhopal, IIFM (Bhopal), National Law Institute University (Bhopal), Institute Of Engineering & Science IPS Academy Indore, All India Institute of Medical Sciences Bhopal, Jabalpur Engineering College, Ujjain Engineering College, Madhav Institute of Technology and Science, Gwalior and Shri Govindram Seksaria Institute of Technology and Science.

IIITDM Jabalpur

Administration Block Institute Of Engineering & Science IPS Academy

The state also has a veterinary science university (Nanaji Deshmukh Veterinary Science University) with three constituent colleges at Jabalpur, Mhow and Rewa. First state private university of MP is "Jaypee University Of Engineering & Technology, Guna" build as very beautiful campus on NH-3. JUET is ranked 86 in top 100 as per NIRF.

IITTM, Gwalior - A Pioneer in Tourism Education

There are 500-degree colleges, which are affiliated with one of the universities in the state. These universities include Jawaharlal Nehru Agriculture University, Madhya Pradesh Veterinary Sciences University, Madhya Pradesh Medical Science University, Rajiv Gandhi Technical University (Bhopal), Awadhesh Pratap Singh University (Rewa), Barkatullah University (Bhopal University), Devi Ahilya Vishwavidyalaya(Indore), Rani Durgavati University (Jabalpur), Vikram University (Ujjain), Jiwaji University (Gwalior), Dr Hari Singh Gaur University (SagarUniversity), Indira Gandhi National Tribal University (Amarkantak, Anuppur) and Makhanlal Chaturvedi National University of Journalism and Communication (Bhopal).

The Professional Examination Board was initialised as Pre Medical Test Board by Government of Madhya Pradesh in the year 1970. After some year in 1981, Pre Engineering Board was constituted. Then after, in the year 1982 both these Boards were amalgamated and named as Madhya Pradesh Professional Examination Board (M.P.P.E.B.) also known as Madhya Pradesh Professional Examination board(Old Name was Vyapam).

Universities

- Barkatullah University, Bhopal
- Bhoj University, Bhopal
- Indira Gandhi National Open University, Bhopal
- Makhanlal Chaturvedi National University of Journalism, Bhopal
- National Law Institute University, Bhopal
- Rajiv Gandhi Technical University, Bhopal

- Devi Ahilya Vishwavidyalaya (formerly Indore University)
- RDVV university (Rani Durgavati Vishwavidyalaya), formerly Jabalpur University, Jabalpur
- Doctor Hari Singh Gour University, also known as **University of Sagar**, Sagar

Institutes

- University Institute of Technology of RGPV, Bhopal (Formerly Bhopal Engineering College)
- Maulana Azad National Institute of Technology, Bhopal
- Indian Institute of Forest Management (IIFM)
- Indian Institute of Hotel Management, Bhopal
- Indian Institute of Management Indore*
- Institute of Engineering and Technology (IET) Indore
- Govindram Seksaria Institute of Technical Studies (SGSITS) Indore
- Mahatma Gandhi Memorial Medical College (MGM) Indore
- Institute for Excellence in Higher Education
- Institute of Professional Education and Research (IPER)
- Lakshmi Narain College of Technology (LNCT)
- Netaji Subhash Chandra Medical College, Jabalpur
- Jawaharlal Nehru Krishi Vishvavidyalaya, Jabalpur
- Govt. Model Science College, Jabalpur. Estd 1836 & science degree courses started in 1896.
- Maharana Pratap College of Technology, Gwalior
- IIITM Gwalior
- Indian Institute of Tourism and Travel Management, IITTM, Gwalior
- Lakshmi Bai National Institute Of Physical Education (LNIPE), Gwalior
- Institute of Hotel Management, Gwalior
- Jiwaji University, Institute of Engineering Gwalior (IEJU)
- Indira Gandhi Engineering college, Sagar

Colleges

- All Saints' College of Technology
- Benazir College
- Bhopal Institute of Technology and Science (BITS), Bhopal
- Gandhi Medical College
- Hamidia College
- Kamla Nehru College, Bhopal
- Maharani Laxmi Bai (Girls) College
- Motilal Vigyan Mahavidyalay (Motilal Science College)
- NRI Institute of Information Science and Technology (NIIST)
- Oriental Institute of Science and Technology (OIST)
- RKDF Institute of Science & Technology
- Safia College
- Sagar Institute of Research and Technology (SIRT)
- Sarojini Naidu Girls P.G. College (also known as Nutan College)
- University Institute of Technology, Barkatullah University
- Holkar Science College Indore
- **The Govt. Engineering College (GEC), Jabalpur** (originally named Robertson Engineering College).

Schools

- All Saints School, Idgah Hills, Bhopal
- Cambridge Senior Secondary School, Idgah Hills, Bhopal
- Campion School, Bhopal
- Carmel Convent Senior Secondary School, B.H.E.L, Bhopal
- Delhi Public School Bhopal
- Kamla Nehru Public Higher Secondary School, Bhopal
- Pd. Lajja Shankar Jha Govt. Model Higher Secondary School, Jabalpur

- St. Joseph's co-ed Senior Secondary School, Arera Colony, Bhopal
- St. Joseph's convent Senior Secondary School, Idgah Hills, Bhopal
- Daly College, Indore
- St. Raphael's Girls School, Indore
- St. Paul's Higher Secondary School,
- Sri Sathya Sai Vidhya Vihar (popularly known as Sathya Sai), Indore
- South Indian Cultural Association (SICA) School
- Scindia School, Gwalior
- Carmel Convent School, Gwalior
- Saint Pauls' School, Gwalior
- Scindia Kanya Vidyalaya, Gwalior
- Saint Joseph's Convent School Sagar.
- St. Joseph Convent School, Khandwa.

JAN SHIKSHA KENDRA

A middle school designated as Jan Shiksha Kendra for a cluster of primary & middle schools to act as quality circle to provide:

- Mutual academic support to teachers
- Opportunities for exchange of experiences
- Support schools academically
- Head master of concerned school will be Jan Shiksha Prabhari
- A Jan Shikshak will be designated to coordinate between schools and Jan Shiksha Kendra

Jan Shikshak

Jan Shikshak has to be:

- Upper Division Teacher/Shiksha Karmi grade -2 or 3 (regular)
- D.Ed./B.Ed trained

- Below 50 years in age
- 5 year of teaching experience in school.

Jan Shikshak shall:

- Provide academic support to teachers of primary level
- Provide on the spot guidance to teachers at the time of school visit
- Coordinate training programme of teachers
- Coordinate between school & community
- Review status of educational indicators *viz.* enrolment, attendance, retention & achievement

Janpad Shiksha Kendra

Establishment of Janpad Shiksha Kendra at block level to coordinate activities of elementary education. There shall be a Janpad Shiksha Kendra coordinator and 3 Janpad Academic Coordinators to provide academic support to schools and Jan Shiksha Kendras.

Zila Shiksha Kendra

Zila Shiksha Kendra shall consist of:

- District Collector - Ex - Officio Head
- CEO, Zila Panchayat, to coordinate the functions
- District Adult Education Officer
- District Institute for Education and Training
- District Project Office of Shiksha Mission.

Zila Shiksha Kendra shall coordinate, supervise and support activities of elementary education and total literacy at district level.

JAN SIKSHA ABHIYAN

M.p.jan Shiksha Adhiniyam 2002

First of its kind in the country for ensuring improvement of quality in Government Schools (elementary) through sharing of responsibility. Universalisation of elementary education is a collective endeavour of government and society. The Jan Shiksha

Adhiniyam helps to move forward in this direction. The Act ensures quality education available for all children of Madhya Pradesh.

RIGHTS OF LEARNERS

Every Child in Madhya Pradesh has a right to access elementary education of quality:

- Learners, if they are more than 25 in the tribal areas and 40 in non-tribal areas, have the right to have a primary schooling facility within 1 km of their habitation.
- No child shall be denied admission for elementary education in Government and Local body schools.

If any person prevents a child from accessing education, he or she is punishable Under Section, 4(2).

- Under Section 22 of the Act, the Gram Sabha can impose fine on a parent, who is willfully not sending the child to School.
- The learners have the right to good quality education, this right will be realised through the enhanced commitment of the teachers, academic and managerial support from the government and active involvement of parents.
- No tuition fee shall be collected from any child studying in any Government and Local body school of the state under Section, 6(1).
- Based on the local requirements, school timings and local holidays shall be decided by Parent Teacher Association to facilitate the right to education of children, specially of deprived communities and girls. The Act provides regular monitoring of quality education in schools by Parent Teacher Association.

Rights and Responsibilities of Teachers

Teachers have both rights and responsibilities under the Jan Shiksha Adhiniyam. So far, the teachers were alone in the endeavour of ensuring good education. Now they would have the support of Community and Parents through Parent-Teachers Association in each school.

- Teachers cannot be deputed for non-teaching tasks except with explicit orders of Government from State level (under Section 10). This will provide more time to focus on improving quality of education. Teachers have right for their Professional development [Under Section 25(4)].

Incentives would be given for meritorious teachers.

- Teachers will ensure regular attendance of children in the school.
- Punishment of children in any form is banned.

Teachers will:

- Provide quality and remedial teaching to ensure achievement of children up to a satisfactory level.
- Ensure equitable treatment to all children.
- Present and review the Annual Academic Report (Jan Shiksha Prateevedan) to Parent Teacher Association to ensure transparency.
- Organise PTA meetings every month to consult and review the academic achievement of children and other problems of school.

Rights and Responsibilities of Parents

The Act provides learning facility as per norm, now it is parents responsibility to ensure all children enrolled in school.

Parents have the right:

- To form Parent Teacher Association and elect President, Vice President and Executive Committee.
- To identify suitable persons like retired teachers to contribute their time to teaching in Schools on an honorary basis and enlist them through PTA.
- To see answer sheets of their children in meetings of Parent Teacher Association and to take action to improve situation of weaker children.

- To admit their children in schools in mid-session, in case they migrate to different destinations in course of the year.
- To augment the resources of school through Shala Shiksha Kosh.
- Management of School is the responsibility of Parent Teacher Association.
- Learning Achievement of Children would be reported to PTA in every quarter [under Section 25(3)]
- To ensure regular attendance of teachers and students in school through Parent Teacher Association.

Rights and Responsibilities of Elected Representatives

Management of school and ensuring quality has been brought under the supervision of People's representatives, at school level through PTA, at village level through Gram Sabha, at District level through Zilla Panchayat, Municipal Bodies and Zila Yojana Samiti.

- Jan Shiksha Yojna developed by PTA shall be presented to Gram Sabha at village level and to Zila Yojana Samiti at district level for discussion and approval.
- Provision has been made for discussion of academic reports at the school level in the meetings of PTA, which is a legal entity.
- Provision made for discussion & review of academic records of children on annual basis, through, Annual Academic Report prepared on the basis of Legislative Constituencies and would be placed in the District Planning Committee each year.
- State level Annual Academic Report, giving constituency-wise information on academic status of preceding academic session is to be presented in the winter session of the Assembly each year.
- Performance of teachers to be monitored by the elected representatives through Parent Teacher Association of each school.

Bibliography

Balchin, P., & Kieve, L.: *Urban Land Economics*, London, MacMillan Press, 1977.

Benjamin, J.: *Socio-religious Status of Panchayati Raj in India*, New Delhi, Ashish Publishing, 1991.

Bhargav Arun: *Rural Marketing and Agribusiness in India*, Surendra, Delhi, 2010.

Brijesh Mishra: *Glimpses of Social Welfare in India : Problems and Perspectives*, ABD Pub, Delhi, 2006.

Chaturvedi, Pratima : *Social Work : Theories and Practices,* Book Enclave, Delhi, 2005.

Clough, Richard: *Construction Project Management in Rural India*, New York, John Wiley & Son, 2000.

Dak, T.M.: *Women and Work in Panchayati Raj*, Delhi, Discovery, 1988.

Damon, William: *Social and Rural Development in Indian Villages*, New York, Norton, 1983.

Dennis, L.: *Public Policy Management in Rural India*, New York, Longman, 1999.

Dimson, Elroy: *Rural Market Anomalies*, Cambridge University Press, 1988.

Dornbush, R.: *International Economic Policy,* Baltimore, The Johns Hopkins University Press, 1979.

Downs, Anthony: *An Economic Theory of Democracy,* New York, Harper and Row, 1957.

Ehrenberg, Ronald: *Modern Labor Economics,* Harper Collins, 1994.

Evenett, S. and B. Hoekman: *The WTO and Government Procurement,* Northampton, Edward Elgar, 2006.

Gagan Kumar Singh: *Administration for Rural Development Programmes in India*, Abhijeet, Delhi, 2003.

Gerald D.: *Determining Economic Damages,* Santa Ana, CA: James Publishing, 1995.

Granger, Clive W. J.: *Empirical Modeling in Economics, Specification and Evaluation,* London, Cambridge University Press, 1999.

Greer, Douglas F.: *Industrial Organization and Public Policy,* MacMillan Publishing Company, 1992.

Hallgren, M. H., & McAdams, A. K.: *The Economic Efficiency of Internet Public Goods,* Massachusetts, MIT Press, 1997.

Harrigan, K. R.: *Strategies for Declining Businesses.* Lexington, MA: Heath, 1980

Hart, Oliver: *Firms, Contracts, and Financial Structure,* Clarendon Press, Oxford, 1995.

Hausman, D. M.: *The Inexact and Separate Science of Economics,* Cambridge, Cambridge University Press, 1992.

Hayek, F. A. *Individualism and Economic Order,* The University of Chicago Press, Chicago, 1948.

Huang, Chi-fu: *Foundations of Financial Economics,* Prentice-Hall, 1988.

Hunt, E. K. *History of Economic Thought, A Critical Perspective,* New York, HarperCollins, 1992.

Jack Kemp: *A Monetary Agenda for the World Economy,* Boston, Quantum, 1984.

Jain S.C. : *New Trends in Rural Marketing,* RBSA Pub, Delhi, 2011.

Jeffrey D. Jones: *Handbook of Business Valuation,* New York: Wiley, 1992.

Judith, E.: *The Sexual Exploitation of Panchayati Raj,* Cambridge, Polity Press, 1986.

Kamble, N. D.: *Deprived Castes and their Struggle for Equality,* Ashish Publishing House, New Delhi, 1983.

Kelly, F. P.: *Charging and Accounting for Bursty Connections,* Massachusetts, MIT Press, 1997.

Kieve, L.: *Urban Land Economics,* London, MacMillan Press, 1977.

Loomes, G.: *Current Issues in Microeconomics,* New York: St. Martin's Press, 1989.

Martin, Gerald D.: *Determining Economic Damages,* Santa Ana, CA: James Publishing, 1995.

Index

B

Bandhavgarh National Park, 69, 74, 90, 140, 148, 149.

C

Compensatory Management, 86.
Craftsmanship, 30, 31, 122, 123, 156, 161, 162.
Custom Hiring Services, 45, 46.
Customs, 17, 25, 28, 141.

D

District Functionary, 45.

F

Folk Dance, 36.
Folk Music, 21, 22, 33, 34, 35.
Forest Composition, 82.
Forest Growing Stock, 83.
Forest Produce, 96, 99, 115, 116.
Forest Statistics, 71.
Fort Ahilya, 29.
Funding Mechanism, 90.

G

Gandhi Sagar Dam, 79.

I

Industry, 2, 18, 68, 97, 99, 100, 102, 103, 104, 107, 108, 119, 120, 122, 123, 124, 125, 132, 134, 154, 162, 163.
Information Technology, 49, 101, 118.
Infrastructure, 87, 90, 103, 116, 118, 131, 133, 135, 141, 147.

K

Kanha National Park, 69, 74, 84, 140, 149, 150.

L

Legislative Assembly, 49, 55, 56.
Lok Sabha Elections, 53.

M

Monsoon Season, 23.

N

National Horticulture Board, 133.

National Parks, 69, 70, 74, 75, 83, 84, 88, 89, 138, 140, 143, 147.
Natural Areas, 74.
Nature Reserves, 70, 140.

P

Payment of Tax, 110.
Pench National Park, 70, 74, 76, 140, 150, 151.
Predominant Languages, 60.
Prospective Investors, 115.

R

Reservoir Data, 77.
Rivers, 3, 16, 34, 62, 65, 68, 91, 92, 93, 94, 178.

T

Traditions, 17, 23, 25, 28, 123, 163, 176.

V

Vidhan Sabha Elections, 54.

W

Wildlife Conservation, 86, 148.
Wildlife Wing, 85, 91.

❑❑❑